FLYING UNDER ᵀʰᵉ RADAR

Tony Inwood

U K Book Publishing.com

Design, typesetting and publishing by UK Book Publishing

www.ukbookpublishing.com

ISBN: 978-1-916572-52-2

FLYING UNDER THE RADAR

Preface

In the writing of this book, I have drawn from a number of sources, other than my current memories. Firstly, and especially for the very early years, from 39 pages of text that my mother wrote about life on Coldridge Farm in order to support her case for divorce.

Secondly from the childhood files kept on my brother and me by the local authority and the Caldecott Community Children's Home, (now Foundation). Indeed, there are some chapters where I have included large extracts directly from these files, as I feel they illustrate the situation with foster parents and holiday problems far more clearly than I can myself and most importantly give a professional perspective. However, I have omitted details of the identities of the professionals involved, as well as the name of the local authority concerned.

Finally, from my own recorded memories. These are contained in an unpublished manuscript which I wrote over 40 years ago. Without these, the book would not really have been possible, as my current memories are far less detailed after such a long passage of time.

I have split the book up into 4 seasons, which reflect the distinct periods of my life so far. I also include some poems that I have written to help illustrate or highlight different aspects of the story.

One of the aims of this book is to try and understand a little more about myself and the people who have played a significant role in my childhood, in as far as that is humanly possible. For how can we ever really know and understand the truth about ourselves, or others and be completely objective? Nonetheless, I have sought to present as balanced and accurate a picture as I can, by seeking to pull together into one meaningful whole, all the complex strands of my life. To any extent that I may have succeeded, I give thanks and praise to Almighty God.

As is clear from this autobiography, my own childhood was not an easy one by any standards. However, it does not really begin to compare with the appalling lives experienced by far too many young people today. We need only to hear about the terrible plight of children in war zones and refugees, whose lives have been torn apart. Here at home, there are those who are sucked into the drug and gang culture, with its attendant knife crime. There are also those who have suffered horrendous sexual and physical abuse from adults, sometimes at the hands of their own parents.

If I can achieve just one thing with this book, it is to highlight the damaging effects of a disturbed childhood in detail, in order to bring into sharp focus the crucial need for children to be brought up in a loving and nurturing environment.

My hope and prayers are that where this cannot be the case, help and healing can be brought about in a way that enables damaged children to become functional again, and to live at least reasonably happy and productive lives. May all organisations such as children's charities and social services have all the resources they need, to help bring this about.

Tony Inwood.

24th September 2023.

Acknowledgements

To my brother, Colin, who went to great lengths to obtain copies of our childhood files from various sources and type up details from some of the old microfiche files that were not always easy to read. This engendered much in the way of mutual exploration of our past, which proved to be highly beneficial to us both and of great value in assisting with the writing of this book.

To my dear friend, Simon, who has played such an important part in my life over so many happy and stable years. His warmth, optimistic character and loyalty have brought me much in the way of stimulation, joy and regeneration. We also have many good and varied friends, which is wonderful.

To the Rev'd Dr. Richard Moy, who has so kindly taken a great interest in my story and offered so much in the way of encouragement. He has also written the Foreword to this book.

Finally, I have found so much of real value in my Christian faith and the years that I have been a member of my local Church have brought me many blessings. My experience of healing prayer has helped to dramatically transform my perceptions about life in general and enabled me to review my past in a positive and life enhancing way. So, for all these enormous improvements in my life I offer grateful thanks to a loving and merciful God.

Foreword

Some years ago, I sat with Tony to interview him for my degree. Tony explained his life and history so naturally that I was quickly caught up in his story. What was most striking was the way he could see God intervening through various people at key moments of his life and the moving depth of relationship he had found with God.

Tony is able to bring together the story of a past that few people would ask for, with a hope for a future that everyone is longing for. He integrates that in his presence with charm, forgiveness, grace, humility and reconciliation. He has had some key moments of breakthrough, but, as a good gardener he knows it is the consistent care of our spiritual lives that in the long-term makes the difference, not just those 'aha' moments when a lot of weeds get cleared away in one go.

Tony is an incredible man with an undoubted warmth and genuine Christian spirit. I would commend this book to anyone, but perhaps especially to those who are looking for the possibility of hope that there is a way to overcome adversity.

Rev'd Dr. Richard Moy. National Director SOMA UK, Associate Vicar Christ Church W4.

Timeline

Born on Coldridge Farm	30-11-52
Left Coldridge Farm	8-6-59
Cope Hall	8-6-59 to 26-5-60
Sunnyside Foster Home	26-5-60 to 20-6-60
Reception/Assessment Centre	20-6-60 to 10-1-61
Caldecott Community Children's Home	10-1-61 to July 69

(Term time only) including:

The Paddocks	1963 to 1965
Lacton Hall	1965 to 1967
The Colt House	1967 to 1969
The holiday Foster Home	1961 to 1967
Toc H. Hostel London, flat in Charing.	July 69 to Oct 71

and various bedsits, including spells of sleeping rough.

The move to East Sheen.	Oct 71 to March 72
Flat in Shepherds Bush	March 72 to Oct 72
House in West London	Oct 72 to present day.

Dedication

This book is dedicated to those children whose experience of childhood may have been less than desirable and especially those for whom it has been disastrous. May they all find comfort, healing and peace.

Earthquake

They are not dead,
but buried.
If you listen carefully
you can hear their
faint cries,
echoing.

The building blocks
of life hardly began,
before the architect's
blueprint was destroyed.

Can we find them
sitting in the
broken dreams of unbuilt
buildings?

Skyscraper potential
stuck in its foundations.

AUTUMN

Autumn

I listen to the wind
in the trees.
The days are growing
ever shorter.

Leaves flutter
all around me
to lie,
inevitably,
on the ground
and decay slowly.

Hopes start to
fade
into the twilight.

Chapter 1
In the Beginning

This story starts and ends with my parents. Why would it begin with anything else? They brought me into being me after all. But into being what?

I was born on a farm in the early 1950s. My father had come from a farming background and all his brothers and his sister became farmers too. Their parents were tenant farmers on a farm called "Ridgemoor", in Burghclere, Hampshire, which was then owned by Lord Porchester, but is now owned by Lord Andrew Lloyd-Webber as part of his Sydmonton Court Estate.

My great, great Grandfather, Daniel Inwood, had been a wealthy farmer. He had a son, Daniel Junior, who apparently had an affair with a live-in-maid who became pregnant by him. Daniel senior was said to have told his son to disown the maid, but Daniel Junior refused to do so and married her. They then had more children, including my grandfather.

Consequently, it appears that Daniel Senior cut his son out of his will and left his money to charity. This included a large sum to help build a cottage hospital in Alton, Hampshire, which was named "The Inwood Cottage Hospital" in recognition of this.

Daniel Senior had wanted his son to become a chemist and sent him to London to train for that profession. However, Daniel Junior's real ambition was to carry on farming. I have a letter from Daniel Senior, written in classic Victorian style, to his son, which shows just what was expected of him. So, it was a kind of irony that by being disinherited, Daniel Junior did indeed get his heart's desire in the end. He thus became a tenant farmer, presumably with an eye to economy, having started off more or less from scratch.

My mother's background was rather different to this. She was born in 1918 of a family that was indirectly descended from George Canning (on her mother's side), who was for a short time Prime Minister of this country. He also held several other important posts, including that of Foreign Secretary.

Her mother had married twice, her second husband was Sydney Boyes, a sculptor of some note. He produced many statues and busts in his lifetime, one of which was sold to Queen Mary. He also sculpted a life size statue of

Lord Leighton, which graces the front of the Victoria and Albert Museum in Kensington.

The V&A evolved in various guises and locations over many years, its immediate forerunner was the South Kensington Museum. The famous Victorian architect, Sir Aston Webb, was commissioned to design the main entrance building in Cromwell Road and the laying of the foundation stone for this by Queen Victoria, was on 17th May 1899. It was then that it was re-named the Victoria and Albert Museum. My grandfather was commissioned by Sir Aston Webb, along with various other sculptors, to create statues for the front of this building. When it was completed, it was opened by King Edward VII and Queen Alexandra on 26th June 1909 and my grandfather was invited to the occasion.

Although the home atmosphere was a reasonably happy one, the family were always rather short of money. So, this coupled with the fact that my grandmother was always in a rather delicate state of health, meant that the social life of the family was more or less non-existent, which couldn't exactly have helped my mother to develop much in the way of friends and social skills. In addition to this my grandmother had a rather domineering personality. My mother, too, was very strong willed and this led to rows developing between them. So eventually my mother decided to leave the family home and join the ATS, partly to get away from her mother.

It was during this time that she met up with a Canadian soldier during the war, whom she then married and had two children by him. Soon after the war, though, he deserted her and went to Australia. So, there she was, having been de-mobbed, with two small children, no husband and no job. So, she moved back with her parents and took a clerical job. After a while though, her parents decided to move to a different part of the country and my mother was forced to find her own accommodation. This was not easy, being a single mother with two small children. To add to her troubles, her eldest son, Glen, was now displaying behavioural problems as he, sadly, had been brain damaged at birth. Consequently, he had to be placed in an institution, where he spent the rest of his life.

Meanwhile, she also had to place her second son, Dennis, into a Barnardo's home in order to find a place to live. However, after a while she found that she couldn't bear to be away from him and realising that he must be suffering emotionally, decided to take a job as a live-in housekeeper, so that she could be with him all the time.

Unfortunately, this situation did not work out very well, so in November 1947 she answered an advert in her local paper which read *"Companion/help required for an elderly farmer's wife"*. She promptly applied for the post and got it. The elderly farmer's wife in question was my father's mother, the job was at Ridgemoor and this is how my mother and father met.

My father, who was 40 years old at the time, was still unmarried and very devoted to his mother. Apparently, he was a bit of a mummy's boy, and probably used to getting his own way for much of the time. He was also very highly-strung. So much so, in fact, that he tended to get worked up about things very easily and was given to shouting a lot, even when he was pleased about something. Consequently, his parents were constantly ticking him off about this. When his mother died within a few months of my mother arriving at Ridgemoor, he was devasted. So, too, was his father, who started to drink very heavily as a result, and consumed a good deal of whisky in his final years.

My mother decided to stay on as housekeeper, though, which on the whole proved to be a satisfactory situation for her, except when my grandfather was the worse for drink and would criticise her work un-necessarily. He threatened to sack her on more than one occasion, but fortunately my father would always stand up for her, saying that if she went, he too would leave and this always defused the situation.

My grandfather, in his depression, would go out drinking most evenings, with my Uncle Jack, leaving my mother and father alone in the house together. After a while their relationship began to develop and my mother who was by then 30 years old, with two small children, one of whom was mentally retarded, was beginning to feel that her prospects of marriage and a secure financial future looked very bleak.

So, this, along with the increasing attraction she and my father had for each other, meant that despite various precautions, she became pregnant. However, when my father discovered this, he was furious and insisted that she should go to the doctor and ask for an abortion. He also suggested that she should hint to the doctor that she might commit suicide if she didn't get one. So, in a somewhat tormented state she went to see her doctor. Fortunately, he refused point blank to give her an abortion and as a result, my brother, Colin, was born nine months later.

When my grandfather learned of the situation, he told my father that he should make plans to marry my mother just as soon as the divorce from her first marriage came through. Thus, in January 1949 they moved to a small farm nearby. This had been bought by my grandfather and some of it had been given as a gift to my father. The rest came in the form of a loan, for which he had to pay back some money on a regular basis, although the exact arrangement is not entirely clear.

Two months later the wedding took place in a registry office. It was not attended by any relatives from either side of the family, the witnesses being the registrar's clerk and a solicitor. The latter then came back to the farm afterwards for a cup of tea and that was all there was in the way of a reception. There were no drinks, no wedding cake and no honeymoon.

Chapter 2
Setting up Home

The farm that my parents had moved to was quite small, totalling only 59 acres of land. The house was very damp and draughty, there was no hot water and the WC was just an earth closet outside. There was no bathroom either and this must all have seemed extremely primitive to my mother, after her town upbringing and a complete contrast to what she had been used to. She hadn't really taken to the idea of living on a farm at Ridgemoor in the first place, but at least the conditions there had been reasonable. This new situation was rather different.

So, they began to furnish the house as best they could. My mother had no money at all to speak of, so it was down to my father to provide virtually everything. Even the few wedding gifts they had received came from his side of the family. So, after all the furniture had been bought, it still left the house a little bare and empty. However, as time went on my father bought more furniture and carpets and my mother's parents gave them some items of furniture too.

Later on, they had a bath and flush toilet installed, but there was still no hot water and very little heating. Money was still really tight as well and after all this had been done, my father had only a small amount of capital left over, which he needed to run the farm and maintain a wife and two children. He also, of course, had to re-pay some of the interest on a loan his father had taken out to buy the farm in the first place. Clearly, he had to be extremely careful with money just to survive. So, almost inevitably, this meant that the housekeeping money that my mother received was inadequate.

As a result, she found it to be a struggle to make ends meet. Whenever clothes wore out, she had to mend them time and again at my father's insistence, which she accepted at first. However, as time wore on and the financial situation improved, the housekeeping allowance didn't. So there arose a degree of friction between them over these issues and they began to quarrel.

I think my father was right to be prudent in the early days of living on the farm as security for the family and making the farm pay was paramount. He even managed over time to make very significant improvements to the very basic living conditions that he inherited. However, he did have a mean streak where finances were concerned and his careful management of funds to begin with, I believe, got out of hand over the years by his refusal to spend money in a reasonable way, when things improved.

So, my mother was justified to some degree in her position over money, but there were, as is so often the case, faults on both sides. However, there were other things that occurred too, which my mother was unhappy about in the early stages of life on the farm. For instance, on their first Christmas together she bought him a present, but he gave her nothing in return. When she mentioned this to him later in the day, he apparently expressed surprise that she should even expect one. Also, when she was pregnant with my brother, Colin, he expected her to perform heavy tasks and other work right up to the afternoon when she went into the nursing home to give birth.

This situation continued for about three years and showed no signs of ever changing and this began to wear my mother down. The rows increased in intensity, and she began to have migraine attacks. So, as sometimes happens in marriage, she thought that if they had another child, it might bring them closer together and that gradually they could work things out. So, two months later, I was on the way.

Sadly, tragedy then struck, as my father had a cerebral haemorrhage.

During the time that he spent in hospital, my mother had to take care of everything on the farm. She had some help from my father's nephew, who presumably took care of the farm labouring, but she had to make all the decisions. This was as well as looking after the children and visiting the hospital, all while she was still pregnant with me.

Apparently when she visited the hospital, my father would be critical of the decisions she had made and blamed her for his illness, saying that it was her incessant nagging that had brought on his haemorrhage in the first place.

Now, without wishing to excuse my father's attitudes and behaviour, I will say in his defence that my mother could be very forcible in her dealings with people. Indeed, my own experience of her on occasions, showed that she could be extremely self-willed and even destructive at times. Once again, faults on both sides.

Fortunately, my father made a full recovery from his illness and returned to full time work on the farm. However, the rows continued. Three months later, I was born.

Chapter 3
Life on the Farm

Of the three of us children, I think my brother Dennis had the hardest time. This was partly because he was older and therefore more was expected of him by my father in terms of helping out on the farm. This was probably not too uncommon for farm life in the 1950s, but I think he was over-used. However, my father would praise Dennis, on occasions when he did things well, and later on when Dennis was older, agreed to pay him for certain tasks like cleaning up the yard.

So, from the age of 8, a typical day for Dennis meant rising at 6am getting dressed in his school uniform of shorts and blazer, putting on his wellington boots and accompanying my father out onto the farm to round up the cows for milking. After that they would come in for breakfast. Then after school, there would be more help needed.

I was too young to remember much of the details of life on the farm, although I do have some very clear personal memories. However, after we left and my mother entered into divorce proceedings, she wrote a very comprehensive, if not a little overblown, at times, account of what life was like. So, I have drawn fairly heavily on this in order to paint as true a picture as I can of the reality.

Breakfast, apparently, consisted of a bowl of cereal, with the milk watered down in order to make it go further. My father would only allow us one pint of milk a day between the five of us. Also, my mother was only allowed to cook two eggs at breakfast and he always had one, so the rest of us took it in turn to have the second one.

All the water that we used on the farm was metered, so to save money my father rarely used the water cooler for the milk when he put it into the churns. Sometimes the dairy would send back a churn that had gone sour and far from being thrown away, we were expected to consume as much as possible that day before the remainder was given to the pigs. In addition to this, occasional broken eggs that were scraped up from the chicken house floor were meant to be consumed first, before fresh ones could be used. Invariably, he was the only one willing to eat the dirty eggs and drink the sour milk, so the rest of us had to go without for the day.

As Dennis grew older, in addition to helping round up the cows, he was expected to clean out the cowsheds and pigsties too, morning and evening. Sometimes he was kept away from school, to help out on the farm as well. My father had employed proper labourers at one point, but because of disagreements over wages and conditions, they had all left.

One summer, a lorry came to the farm to deliver some animal foodstuffs. Dennis, who was helping to unload it, was standing by as it reversed towards the barn. The driver stopped, but kept the engine running as he actually intended to reverse again. Dennis not realising this, however, started to climb onto the back of the lorry, just as the driver started reversing. My father shouted at the driver, who stopped at once, but not before the lorry had pinned Dennis against the open door of the chicken house. As it was, he fell onto the floor of the chicken house and lay there groaning in agony.

My father and the driver, meanwhile, proceeded to unload the lorry. This took about 20 minutes and it was only after that time that they carried Dennis indoors and placed him in an armchair. Then, when the lorry had gone, my father rang the doctor after some insistence from my mother. Some considerable time later, Dennis was taken to hospital and was found to be suffering from a fractured pelvis.

He was in hospital for four weeks. I do actually remember visiting him then with my mother and Colin. We took him some toffees, which he enjoyed. It was a brief period of respite for Dennis, though, being in hospital. He was in the men's ward and as he was the youngest there, they all made a bit of a fuss of him. He subsequently told me that as he got better, he got around the ward a little and started to indulge in some minor high-jinx to wind up the other patients. When the time came for him to leave, he burst into tears and told my mother that he didn't want to have to go back to the farm.

Many years later Dennis was in hospital again suffering from blackouts. When he told me this, I couldn't help but see an awkward irony in it.

Milk

"Wroughton" was written
on the label.
"I was in hospital there once", he said.
"Blackouts".
They couldn't find the cause.
"Stress", I thought.
Delayed reaction.
Stress does funny things to people.
Except they're not so funny really.

> Getting up early
> on a freezing winter's morning
> from a damp camp bed.
> Still in his short trousers.
> The cows had to be rounded up for milking,
> before breakfast, before going to school.
> Holes in his boots. Wet feet......

> Ironic really. This story from a bottle of milk.
> From a farm.

Meanwhile, life on the farm continued, as usual, but it wasn't all doom and gloom. In retrospect all three of us do have some happy memories of it too.

There were many simple pleasures to be had. Dennis was very keen on cars and lorries and loved to send off to the manufacturers to get details of their latest models and much enjoyed poring over them. I remember making little cars from empty teabag boxes with sticks put through for axles and cut out cardboard wheels. We used to collect moss and put it in bowls and put in twigs for trees and add water to make miniature landscapes.

I was also not short of toys. I had a pedal car, a scooter and some smaller toys too. One was a farm, complete with plastic animals and another was a garage with toy cars, also a big, polythene, old style locomotive engine. I think some of these may have been bought for me by my Aunt Evelyn, who was also my Godmother, and I clearly recall on one birthday, her sending me a lovely bright red toy wheelbarrow, which gave me a lot of pleasure. However, some were undoubtedly bought by my mother from the money she earned from running a mail order club. She did this to supplement the household allowance and to buy herself the occasional new dress.

Some of the more positive aspects of living on the farm too, were things like playing in the hay bales in the barn. Dennis and Colin once hollowed out a little camp consisting of a tunnel leading to a "Room" at the end. It was always nice to have animals all about us too, and we each chose a cow and named it as our own. Occasionally my dad would give us rides on Nobby, the old carthorse, after he had been put out to grass. After feeling a little nervous to begin with being up so high, after reassurance, I happily looked down on the back of old Nobby's big brown head, as he gently clopped a few yards across the field and back again.

I remember, too, walking across the field with my dad and through the woods on occasions, as he collected firewood. In fact, I used to follow him practically everywhere, when he was milking the cows, doing the garden, or general tasks around the farm. Occasionally his sense of fun would show through, too. He had a walking stick made from an old bit of root. When we asked him why he needed it, he would wink and say that it was because he had a bone in his leg!

He used to love horse racing, although he rarely bet more than a few pennies on a race. When he watched it on TV, he would get very excited if his horse looked like it was going to win. He would then get his imaginary whip out and start "whipping" the side of his armchair! If it did win, he would be absolutely thrilled and re-live the glory by vividly describing the last moments of the race, repeatedly, and saying how well he had "ridden" his horse!

He also used to sing songs to himself whilst he washed eggs in the kitchen or shaved after breakfast. "The Floral Dance" and "The Lord is my Shepherd" were his favourites.

In the summer months we used to have tea in the garden, with bread, cheese, celery and other things and I really loved these occasions. It was such a nice way to enjoy summer evenings.

Christmas Day at the farm was also enjoyable. My mum would buy the presents, and my dad would fill a stocking with an apple, an orange, a small jar of sweets, a sugar mouse, a chocolate Father Christmas and a penny. My dad really seemed to get into the spirit of Christmas, because he would also dress up as Santa Claus, (after a fashion!), to lay the stockings on our beds. I remember during Christmas dinner, the ceremonial pulling of the wishbone from the turkey, too!

Chapter 4
Visits to Relatives

Life on the farm was punctuated with visits to relatives, which were something of a distraction. We also had the odd day trip to the seaside, getting up very early to catch a coach to Swanage or Hayling Island. My mother always took a packed lunch with various items in it including corned beef sandwiches, which I enjoyed. My dad, in classic 50's style, would roll up his trouser legs and paddle in the sea and on the whole it was fun. We never had a proper holiday, though, or went to the cinema or circus or indeed any other form of entertainment. The only exception to this was going several times each year to fetes in surrounding villages. Dennis and Colin would enter races and sports activities like high jump and even apple bobbing. I was too young for that, but I do have a vague memory of being in an egg and spoon race once. My dad would be really pleased if we won anything, because the prizes were not rosettes, but money!

Of the trips to relations, most of them were to those on my dad's side of the family. We used to go to Ridgemoor from time to time to visit my grandfather, most notably on Boxing Day each year. This was a very jolly affair attended by my uncles too. I remember us sitting round the dining room table eating a huge Christmas dinner. The whole scene was so cheerful and festive, with a blazing log fire in the hearth, the Christmas tree laden with presents and all the balloons and other decorations festooned over the walls and ceilings.

My uncle George, who was a very jolly character, would take a balloon and rub it on his hair, for static, and then stick it to the wall. We were amazed and gazed in awe at this balloon stuck up so high, as if by magic. Later on, we were given balloons to play with. I was delighted and chased all around the dining room table, excitedly pursuing them. One accidentally got too near the fire and popped and Uncle George then proceeded to pop a few more for fun, laughing uproariously as he did so!

Ridgemoor was an old rambling Manor House, with a terrace along the side, green shutters on all the windows and two life-size statues of Spaniels on either side of the front door. The garden was quite large and had one prominent feature in that the lawn by the side of the house was composed of three separate tiers of grassy banks. There were also several clumps of majestic pampas grass, which used to fascinate me. On our visits in the summer months, we always had great fun running up and down these banks, having races to see who could get up and down them first. I remember nagging my dad to join in with us once and he reluctantly agreed to begin with, but then got into the spirit of it all and quite enjoyed it.

Inside, the house had a character all of its own with a slightly mysterious quality about it. This was heightened by the dimly lit corridors and the rickety stairs at the back. To a young child it all seemed rather strange and for a long time I firmly believed that Charles Dickens lived in a little room at the top of the back stairs. It was only much later that I found out that it was actually the old, bearded gardener, who went by the name of "Dickens" and lived on the premises.

I never had much to do with my grandfather. I recollect that he used to sit in his armchair by the fire, dressed in a black suit and waistcoat, which sported a gold watch and chain. His walking stick would be propped up beside his armchair and in his hand would be a glass, presumably filled with whisky. Whenever he got up, it always seemed like a great effort for him. He was by that time in his late seventies and not very fit. He died at the age of eighty in 1957, greatly missed by my dad, who was extremely fond of both of his parents. I have a feeling he might have been rather too dependent on them in some ways. After all, he never left home to get married till he was forty.

Then there were the two old springer spaniels, one called Monte and the other, Nelson, who was blind in one eye.

I have a fairly mish-mash recollection of these visits to relatives, but I can certainly recall them with a fair degree of clarity and some would have taken place when I was older, after we had left the farm.

I think my favourite relation was Uncle George as he was so full of life and very welcoming. He and my Auntie Betty used to lay on fabulous teas for us. There was always plenty of bread and butter, thinly sliced with a choice of brown and white. To go with this, we had fish paste and assorted jams, also radishes and seasonal salads. Then to follow we had cakes, biscuits, marshmallows and chocolate fingers and far from having to be polite and eat only modest amounts, Uncle George would cajole us into eating more and more, being very surprised that we had such small appetites. My father, too, was always delighted for us to fill ourselves up at other people's expense!

Uncle George also had an old-fashioned gramophone and would play popular records, which all added to the cheerful atmosphere. I remember, especially, a delightful little song called "Sing Little Birdie" by Pearl Carr and Teddy Johnson.

After tea we boys would go out and play in the farmyard, with our cousin, Michael, who had an air pistol. He and

Dennis would take pot shots at tin cans and Colin and I would wander around looking at all the animals and chatting to the farm hands. Happy memories.

Uncle Harry, the oldest of my uncles, was a somewhat strange character. He was not in the best of health, suffering, as he did, from chronic breathing problems. He was also very fond of drink! He had two little dogs, a Dachshund and a black and white Jack Russell called Badger!

His wife, Auntie Phyllis, was a rather large lady with a bright red face who was always very cheerful. She was most welcoming when we visited and used to provide us with simple, but wholesome food to eat. She had a rather high-pitched, somewhat strangulated voice, which she used most effectively when dealing with my uncle's more unusual characteristics. He used to refer to her either as mother or mummy, according to his mood and clearly depended on her a good deal.

Uncle Harry, probably as a result of the alcohol that he consumed, was a bit of philosopher in his own way and would often tell us stories with great gusto, tending to ramble on rather at times! All of these breathless, throaty ramblings, would be punctuated every few minutes by a quick blast on his inhaler, as he would fight for breath in between sentences! He would pass on quite happily from one long ramble to another, unless, thankfully, checked rather sharply by Auntie Phyllis.

On occasions he would merrily boast of his great love of funerals. It didn't matter to him whether he had known the deceased or not. For some reason he felt an overwhelming desire to be present. I'm not sure if that was to pay his last respects, or because of the free drinks at the reception afterwards. Whatever it was, he was inordinately proud of his record of attending some 60 funerals altogether. The last one the poor soul attended was his own.

Another of my father's relations that we used to visit was my Auntie Evelyn, who was also my Godmother. She and my father were very close, in some ways, being the two youngest members of the family. He always held her in very high esteem and whenever we were with her, he would speak in very reverential tones, almost as though she were royalty! She, like my father, was inclined to be a bit mean, but not as bad as him. And this, coupled with the fact that she was very formal and somewhat severe at times, made visits slightly awkward. I always found them to be a little stifling.

Teatime with Auntie Evelyn was a very genteel affair and one had to be careful not to put a foot wrong! To her credit, the food was always of quality and in reasonably good supply. On one occasion, however, either Colin or I had the great misfortune to spill some cream over the tablecloth. She was furious and scolded us for several minutes, declaring it to be a "wicked waste", to which my father looked on suitably grieved.

Evelyn had married into a very well-off local farming family, but her husband, Uncle John, had very sadly had a severe stroke some years earlier and was basically chairbound. He only had use of one arm and one of his legs was in an iron, in order to help him walk. We always greeted him politely and he would just sit and smoke cigars in front of the fire. He was unable to speak properly and made sort of grunting sounds when he wanted something and somehow my aunt always managed to work out what he was saying and helped him out. I'm sure the years of looking after him, which she did very well, must have been a great strain on her, both physically and emotionally. Added to that, their son, Henry, had tragically died very young when a tractor he was driving along a sloping field, overturned and crushed him to death.

Towards the end of her life she mellowed considerably and later visits to her when we had grown up were much more pleasant affairs.

My memories of my Uncle Jack are very few. He was rather taciturn and never really interacted with us children at all, as far as I remember.

Visits to my mother's relatives were far less frequent. I can recall one such visit when I was very young to see my grandmother after my grandfather (of whom I have no recollection at all) had died. She lived in a house that has been designed by her son, my uncle Marcus, who was an architect. She was very old and frail at that stage and had cancer. My auntie Beryl who had never left home for any length of time, took it upon herself to nurse my grandmother in her final years. On that visit we apparently arrived late and I was very tired. I vaguely remember catching a glimpse of my grandmother sitting propped up in her bed in a darkened room, but not being allowed to go in and see her, as she was too ill.

On subsequent visits over the years, I found that the atmosphere of the house was not particularly congenial. It always struck me as being slightly austere, with its Victorian furniture and dimly lit rooms. I always felt a sense of relief when going out into the garden with its narrow strip of lawn and two apple trees at the end.

Chapter 5
Daily Farm Life

Back on the farm, life continued with visits to relatives being more in the nature of a side-show than anything else. A typical day would see my father tramping around the house often with dung on his boots and occasionally carrying a dead chicken or rabbit. These would then be boiled in a cast-iron pot on the living room fire, fur feathers and all.

When they were cooked, they would be given to the dog. During the summer, when there was no fire, they would be given to the dog raw, and if rejected, would be placed before them again and again. They would also be fed on bread that had gone stale.

The cats were expected to survive by killing mice or rats around the farm (perhaps a not too uncommon a practice on farms in the 1950s). However, my mother would sometimes put out bread and food scraps for them to supplement this. Apparently, two or three cats died over the years and innumerable litters of kittens and were then just thrown onto the dung heap.

One of the dogs died prematurely through neglect. It suffered from time to time with a complaint that required veterinary attention, but my father never took him to the vet, but just mentioned it if the vet called to treat a cow. Presumably, he hoped the vet would treat the dog without any further charge.

I certainly have a clear memory myself of bread being fed to a spaniel we had called Vick. One morning my dad called me into the kitchen and pointed through the open door to the dog in his kennel. He turned to me and said, "You see old Vick, dear, he looks as though he's sleeping, doesn't he?" I looked up at him slightly puzzled and nodded. Well, I'm afraid he's dead", he said gently, "but he looks so peaceful, you wouldn't know it would you?"

I think he was trying to be kind to me by breaking the news gently, but how strange that he should be sensitive to my feelings, but seemingly had no real feeling or empathy for the dog.

Apparently, he could be cruel to his other animals. He used to overwork, Nobby, the carthorse, by making him pull a two-horse chain harrow by himself. As a result of doing this and pulling other heavy loads year after year, the horse developed a bare patch on its back where all the hair had worn way.

On one occasion, Nobby had been pulling a cart loaded with hay bales. However, because my father had not spent money on proper harnessing, but instead used thick string, it broke, causing the shafts to fly upwards forcing the horses head backwards. Thankfully my father managed to pull down the shafts and disentangle the horse, but it could have caused a nasty injury and need never have happened if the right equipment had been used in the first place.

Sometimes, when my father was milking the cows, he would hit them in the face if they did not get properly into position and once one had a swollen eye because of this.

There were other instances of deprivation in domestic life in the treatment of us children. For example, I don't recall very much in the way of physical affection from my mother. She would kiss us, I think, from time to time when going to school and so on, but I don't remember her cuddling us, or any real physical contact. My mother's attentions, as I recall, lacked any real warmth. This may have been partly because of the stress she was under, or perhaps just a part of her personality. Nonetheless, I do have warm memories of her singing songs to us from time to time, one of which was the lovely child's song

"Horsey, Horsey, Don't You Stop".

My dad, on the other hand, could be affectionate. I remember sitting on his knee and sucking my thumb, whilst he would read me a children's story called "Ant and Bee" and he would make various noises throughout the text, such as a motor car, which I much enjoyed. He also used to say, "How much do you love me?" He would then make a measurement between his fingers and say, "That much?" and then hold out his arms and say, "Or that much"? I would shake my head at the latter, just for fun, knowing that he would make a mock hurt and disapproving look. In an odd sort of way, he did actually spoil me for a good part of the time, to the extent that I remained in a rather infantile state for a long time afterwards, which proved to be a hindrance. This is borne out by an educational psychologist's report on me a few years later.

I think it's fair to say that, generally speaking, there was a lack of stimulation for us all, from our parents. I don't recall either of them playing games with us or engaging us much in any activities. This set a pattern, for me at any rate, of a partial withdrawal into myself and I became rather remote and began to live in a kind of imaginary world. This was made worse by the frequent rows they had, which were both painful and frightening. My father at such times scared me and for many years afterwards I always had a rather exaggerated fear of males because of it.

This substantial lack of interest in these areas left me with a deep-seated desire for physical, and emotional warmth. Indeed, this was never really fulfilled for the remainder of my childhood and was something of a handicap in making relationships of any kind later on. In addition to this, I never had any desire to read for pleasure till much later in life and neither did I develop any interests or hobbies.

Over the many years since these events took place, I have been able to look at them somewhat dispassionately and have tried to gain, along with my brother, Colin, a greater understanding of them.

My father was such a strange mixture and had a very complex personality. He was at the very least eccentric, but this was mixed with a degree of emotional warmth which he undoubtedly showed at times. The other side of his nature could be rather frightening when having rows with my mother. This was especially so to a young boy like me, as I could not really get them into the same perspective that an older child or adult would.

For example, during one such row he told my mother that it was his "duty" to murder her. Now I am absolutely certain that he had not got the slightest intention of doing so, but rather was expressing his extreme frustration at my mother who used to goad him. However, I suspect the reason she resorted to goading, is that she may well have felt frustration too, in that she was making very little headway with him over various contentious issues.

I think it's fair to say that their marriage was a classic case of an irresistible force meeting an immovable object, in that my father very largely expected my mother to conform to his view of things, which sometimes may have been justified. Nonetheless, my mother, who was equally strong-willed, was determined not to give in.

I can only conclude that in some ways he was a little divorced from reality and whilst he could undoubtedly be cruel, I am not certain exactly how much was intentional and how much was unconscious on his part. He was definitely mean, but even that was partly tied up with the rather odd views that he had on life generally and the need in the early days on the farm to be careful with spending money. Over the years, I had very mixed feelings for him.

My mother, for all her efforts to try and provide a good home for us, was inclined to be a little panicky and hysterical at times and this, too, made any rows appear more serious to me than perhaps they actually were. She also bore some of the responsibility for what took place overall and later did admit that there were faults on both sides. Having said that, she clearly had a great many hardships, frustrations and difficulties at the farm, with which she had to contend for many years and they did wear her down greatly. I do believe that in many ways she tried her hardest to do the very best for us.

Both my father and mother were Christians, and both, I believe, deeply regretted in later years, much of what took place on the farm and subsequently.

Chapter 6
Leaving Home

Dennis and Colin had been attending school for some time before me. Eventually, though, I was old enough to go to Nursery school and then Primary school. This was all pretty unremarkable really, except in as much as I felt a bit isolated and out of place. I didn't make any friends, and indeed this was substantially true of the three of us children. Dennis had one or two friends who would come back to the farm to play occasionally, but I think that was about it.

Interestingly, neither my father or my mother had any friends either, acquaintances maybe, but not friends. So social life at the farm, apart from visits to relatives, was pretty much non-existent.

I did enjoy colouring pictures and nature lessons in school, though, and one of the highlights for me was the walk back from school with my brothers in the afternoon, through the fields and allotments. At one point this involved crossing a wooden bridge over a little stream. This was over-shadowed by willows and I recall with pleasure the sun filtering down through the trees, and reflecting off the stream, as it bubbled merrily along. Sometimes we would pause a while and throw stones in or just watch the tiny minnows as they darted madly about. Occasionally we would go to the village sweet shop, if we had any money, and buy a bag of pineapple chunks to eat contentedly as we meandered slowly back.

From time to time, we would walk back through the village, which was a bit longer, and Dennis, who always enjoyed playing pranks, would sometimes take the opportunity to ring on people's doorbells and then run off! On one occasion, presumably fresh from an R.E. lesson, he hoisted himself up on a wall and peered inquisitively into the garden beyond it. There he saw a man happily pushing his lawn mower back into the shed and looking very pleased with his afternoon's labours. Dennis then called out to him in his best Biblical tones, "Hast thou finished thy work?" The man apparently looked up slightly startled and upon seeing Dennis, quickly responded, "Dost thou what a clip round the ear?" Dennis clearly didn't, leapt off the wall and ran helter-skelter down the road!

This is how I spent the first six years of my life, with much of it overshadowed by increasing rows and tension between my parents. As each year passed the strain became more apparent in all of us, especially my mother, who was by now at the end of her tether.

Unbeknown to us, and, of course, my father, she had decided, finally, to leave the farm and to take us with her. She had got a part time job after I went to nursery school and had already been running a mail order catalogue for some time prior to this, in order to make enough money to make up the shortfall of food and clothing provided by my father. She also managed to save up some money and she used this to help pay for accommodation for us all after we left.

By this time, her nerves were in such a bad state that she was being prescribed tranquillisers in ever increasing amounts to keep her going. She had decided to leave on a Monday when my father was going out to have lunch with my aunt Evelyn. The day before we left, another furious row broke out between them and appeared so bad to me, that I started hitting my father in an attempt to stop it all. The aftermath of the row snowballed long into the afternoon and evening leaving us feeling miserable.

The next day she saw us off to school in the usual way and then caught the bus to work, later returning to the farm after my father had gone. She had arranged for a removal van to call at midday, presumably to take a few bits of furniture, kitchen utensils and personal belongings away with her. She also ordered a taxi pick her up from the farm and then to pick us boys up from school.

We, of course, were completely unaware of all this activity. Nonetheless, it was from here on that momentous afternoon, that my mother suddenly appeared in my classroom, bundled me and my two brothers into the waiting taxi and told the driver where to take us. Our destination was an old manor house a few miles away called Cope Hall.

Furthermore, as my mother now accompanied us in the taxi, the full impact of what she had done must have come home to her. For there were three children, in that cab, that she now had sole responsibility for. Three very bewildered children, who would now look to her to provide for all their needs.

Chapter 7
Cope Hall

Cope Hall was a fairly large old manor house, set in a few acres of land, with a gravel front drive and a stable block at the back. It was owned by a couple in their early fifties. They occupied one end of the house with their daughter and used the stables and an adjoining paddock from which to run a riding school. Apart from us, there were two other tenants there.

Our accommodation was rather spartan and consisted of one large room downstairs at the front of the house, our own little kitchen down the corridor, and one large bedroom up the first flight of stairs. This was occupied by us children, whilst my mother slept on a divan in the front room.

It was a strange feeling being in a new place. Apart from adapting to the physical environment, I had to adjust to new circumstances emotionally as well. Everything was all of sudden slanted differently. There were no more rows and bad atmospheres. My mother seemed more cheerful and Dennis began to take on the role of joint head of the family with mother. He also got a job, being fifteen by now, and kind of became an adult overnight.

This meant that Colin and I were thrown closer together. It was the beginning of a dependence that I had on him, which lasted for several years.

To begin with I didn't consciously miss my father, or if I did, I didn't really have time to notice it. All I remember was a tremendous feeling of pulling together, fostered by my mother. In a sense she was relying as much on our cooperation, as we were on her care and guidance. It was a very delicate balance and it didn't need very much to upset the scales. Discipline gradually proved to be a problem.

There was still a shortage of money, too, only this time it was simply that my mother didn't have any to speak of. Apart from the little savings she had made at the farm, she was penniless. She relied on the income from her part time job, family allowance and the modest contribution that Dennis was able to make from his wages working as a driver's mate for the local laundry. To start with she didn't receive any maintenance from my father at all.

We did manage to survive on it though and there was a real spirit of working together because we could all feel for mother in her plight. So, we economised wherever we could, albeit in small ways. Colin gave up taking sugar in his tea and we would do things like spreading our bread very thinly with butter.

Within a week of our moving, my father found out our address. He called round and I have a vague memory of mother's panic and horror when she saw him standing at the door. After a week of relative peace, the tension returned. When I saw him framed in the doorway, I felt a mixture of pleasure, as I realised how much I was missing him, but also fear, clearly made worse by my mother's over reaction.

Apparently, he wanted a reconciliation with my mother and when he realised that was not going to happen, he became angry and threatening. Eventually my mother got the landlord to escort him from the premises.

After a while he called again and this time mother only communicated by means of notes with Colin acting as go-between. As a result of this, it was decided that father would have Colin and I back at the farm on alternate weekends. Dennis, however wanted nothing more to do with him.

Over the months that followed, another new form of battle developed between our parents. The difference being that this time the cause of the friction was not so much the principle of our welfare, as the desperate need they each had of our affection and esteem and their desire to spite each other. This was more manifest in my mother than my father though.

This was brought home to me rather forcibly one day when I was in bed with a temperature on the very day that my father had come to visit and take me back to the farm. He accepted, after a while, that if I was ill, then I could not go with him to the farm, but just wanted to come in and spend a short while with me, which I also wanted. Mother, however, was having none of it. So partly through fear of giving him access to the house and partly out of spite barricaded me into the bedroom with her, with the aid of Dennis, in order to deny him entry.

After a while my father realised that he was not going to be able to gain access to the bedroom and retreated down the stairs. As he went away, my heart went out to him knowing how sad he felt at being denied access to his son. I, too, was miserable at not being allowed to see him and whilst I understood my mother's position to some degree, it did seem rather cruel that she should act in this way.

As far as school was concerned, Colin and I had to attend a new one and life there was pretty unremarkable. Colin was in a different building to me, being older, but we did manage to have some contact in break time on the playing fields.

The headmistress of the school had the misfortune to be named Miss Print, and she could be rather strict at times. For example, if anyone did anything wrong, they had to wear a black band and other children were not allowed to talk to them at all during break times.

Once again, I made no friends here. I suppose it was largely because it was only a short time that we were there, as it turned out, so there was no time for any friendships to develop.

Our leisure hours were spent in a variety of ways at Cope Hall. Colin developed an interest in cooking, partly, I think to try and help out mother. So, he would make dishes like macaroni cheese, scones and other little items too.

One thing we much enjoyed when it rained, was going outside into the lane and building a series of dams by the verge using dead leaves mixed with mud and twigs. When the water had built up in the first dam, we would smash it open and watch it rush on down to the next one. This operation would then be repeated for the whole series, and when they had all been broken, we would start the process all over again!

Sometimes, Colin would bully me. On one occasion he and a friend of his from down the lane, tied my hands behind my back and then to a wooden pole. They pushed me over and rolled me into a ditch full of stinging nettles and laughed at me. Then they walked off and said they were going to leave me there till I died. When they finally released me after what seemed like ages, they told me not to tell anyone or it would be all the worse for me.

Life continued in this undulating fashion for nearly a year and as each month passed, mother found it increasingly difficult to cope. The years of living on the farm, followed by having to look after us and do virtually everything by herself meant that she began to suffer from bouts of depression. These became more and more prolonged and the state of her nerves was such that, at times, she found that just having us around her was becoming too much of a strain. On these occasions she was apt to snap and yell at us for practically nothing, and sometimes insisted that we should stay out of the living room altogether if she was eating, as even the slightest commotion upset her.

Her life at work was becoming increasingly difficult for her, too, as she found herself being unable to concentrate properly. Sometimes she couldn't even focus her eyes for reading, seeing only blurred images. She was still taking tranquillisers, but they were not really helping her, even with larger doses.

Then in April 1960, she was given the sack. No actual reason was given, but clearly it was because she was unable to cope with the work. Everything suddenly came to a head and she realised that she was heading for a nervous breakdown. So, she began to negotiate with the Children's Department, in order to have Colin and I placed into care. A month later we were taken to a temporary foster home nearby.

Meanwhile, mother found herself a room and applied for National Assistance (social security). During the months that followed, being relatively free of responsibility, she began to recover and build up her physical strength to the point where in October that year, she obtained a full-time clerical post. She was still dependent on medications at this stage, but was at least able to cope with daily life. After a while she moved again, to a small, but pleasant flat and held down a variety of typing and clerical jobs for some years to come.

Father was still living on the farm at this point and had been able to do so because he had hired a live-in housekeeper to look after the domestic side of things for him. However, after a while, she found him to be rather too difficult to work for and left, leaving him to feel increasingly isolated.

It was now obvious to him that despite his efforts at reconciliation, mother had no intention whatsoever of going back to him. I think a part of him was genuinely shocked and hurt about this, never really comprehending or accepting the significant part that he had played in her departure. Gradually, he too, grew more and more depressed. Without his wife and children around, it seemed pointless to continue working on the farm.

After a while he began to attend the out-patient department of a nearby mental hospital on a voluntary basis, just to keep him going. When he was visited by someone from the Children's Department after Colin and I had gone into care, the children's officer noted that he, too, appeared to be heading for a nervous breakdown. Finally, he decided to sell the farm.

It so happened that around that time his brother George, had just lost his licence and badly needed someone to do the daily milk round. Father seized the opportunity, and gratefully took up residence with Uncle George and Auntie Betty.

Meanwhile, Colin and I were having to face up to our new life in the foster home. The family, by now, was completely disintegrated. All that remained was to see where the pieces had fallen.

Chapter 8
Sunnyside

I felt a good deal of apprehension when we first arrived, with my mother and Dennis, at "Sunnyside", as our new foster home was called. It was a typical 1930s three-bedroomed house with a small garden that had a stream running at the bottom of it. The couple who lived there, who were to be our temporary foster parents, were probably in their early forties. We were introduced to them and then shown around the house. All the time we were being reassured by the adults that we would soon settle in and enjoy it there.

Mother had already explained that she could no longer look after us herself, because of her health, and indeed, the state of her nerves had already impressed themselves upon me. Because of this awareness I accepted, on one level that it had to happen. In another way, though, I resented being left with strangers and despite the reassurances, as the time came for my mother and Dennis to leave, I felt the pain of impending separation welling up inside me, but I controlled my emotions as best as I could. I'm sure Colin did too. I cannot remember distinctly the exact nature of events that evening, but by the time we were alone in our bedroom, I do recall being in desperate need of my mother.

After the initial wrench of being away from both parents as well as Dennis and being placed in another unfamiliar environment so soon after leaving Cope Hall, we slowly began to adjust to our new circumstances. The bond between Colin and I which had really begun to develop at Cope Hall, started to grow even stronger at this point, as we needed each other's support more than ever. The fact that we were still together was the only consistent thing we each had in our lives.

Interestingly, the nature of the relationship between the foster parents in this household was very different to my own parents. Here it was the woman who ran things. This was not in a terribly obvious way, but I could see even at the age of seven, that she was the dominant personality. She was prone to be a little sharp with us and we both found her to be a rather unpleasant woman overall.

The foster father, however, was a kindly man. He was slightly shorter than his wife, rather stocky and had a neatly trimmed moustache. He really seemed to take to us, and we to him, in what turned out to be our short stay there. Fortunately, he helped to make life a little more bearable for us. He once showed us how to make a sort of fishing rod from a long stick, with a length of string and some sort of hook on the end, which we used in the little brook at the bottom of the garden. We never actually caught any fish with it, but it did help to pleasantly pass an hour or so before going to bed.

We had to go to school whilst we were at "Sunnyside", of course, this being the fourth one that we had attended so far. We travelled to it each day by coach. I have no real memories of it, possibly because it transpired that we were only there for such a short time.

Once again, my father found out where we were staying and began to visit us at "Sunnyside". In his dealings with the children's department, they noted in their files (hard to read all the words) that during a telephone conversation with him that:

"Most of the conversation in fact was given over to a tirade against his "wi......(wicked wife?) ..... it was obvious from his remarks that he was concerned far ...... his own feelings than he was about his sons. My impression ..... consumed by self-pity and thoughts of revenge against his wife"

I have only a very hazy memory of his visits, but due to the frequency and nature of these, sometimes at unsocial hours, our foster parents asked the children's department to remove us as quickly as possible. So, 23 days later we were taken away. I was actually quite pleased about this, despite the thought of having to move to yet another unfamiliar location.

The following is another extract from the files held on us by the Children's department. It clearly shows the state of affairs regarding my parents and the foster parents.

Children's Officer's letter to the Clerk of the Council. "The children were received into care on 26 May 1960. Parents separated for just over a year. A long history of matrimonial difficulties, both parents being mentally unstable and full of bitterness towards one another. The admission to care was finally precipitated by a telephone call from Mrs. Inwood's doctor who stated that she was not in a fit state to care for the children. Placed in a very good short stay foster home at no real distance from either parent, where they could continue with their education at their own school in Newbury. However, soon became evident that journey to the school not satisfactory so arrangements made to go to another local school. Both parents informed by letter on 2 June. From the beginning Mr. Inwood created difficulties. Aggressive and sometimes abusive towards the foster parents; visited far more often than they could tolerate, staying until very late at night and dominating the household. A letter was sent to his solicitors on 3 June asking that he should limit his visits to a reasonable number and length of stay. Mr. Inwood took this letter very badly and rang the office demanding that I should personally visit him. I wrote offering him an appointment at the office. He did not attend. On 17 June, following a letter from Mr. Inwood and a visit to him by the Child Care Officer, it was decided to move the children to the county Reception Home. Both parents were immediately notified of this and Mr Inwood expressed his annoyance."

Our next destination, then, turned out to be a Reception Assessment Centre and we were placed there until a suitable long-term establishment could be found for us.

Chapter 9
Oasis

I can't recall arriving at the Assessment Centre, but it was a fairly large house with about 12 bedrooms and set in good-sized grounds. There was a short gravel drive which led up to the front door, with flower beds on either side, a couple of trees and at the end of the drive and a tall hedge, which ran parallel to the pavement. Down on the left-hand side of the house there was a small, wooded area, which could be freely used to play in, and at the back a decent sixed lawn, with another large hedge across the bottom. Behind this hedge there was a vegetable garden and the whole provided plenty of space for recreation. Adjoining the back of the house was a large glass conservatory in which all the children's wellington boots and coats were kept.

The centre was mixed, with about thirty children of varying ages from about four to fifteen years old. There was a school on the premises for all ages run by a male teacher, who also used to supervise games on the back lawn.

The remaining staff, however, were all women and mainly over the age of forty. All of them were known as Auntie this or Auntie that and were all perfectly pleasant. The atmosphere on the whole, was quite a happy one and having settled in, it was very refreshing to be in a relaxed environment, with nice people to look after us. This proved to be something of an oasis in my life and during this period, the memory of my previous bad experiences receded a little.

Fairly soon after we arrived, Colin and I had to see an Educational Psychologist, who also wrote a brief report on each of us in respect to our personal development. This report, of which I have seen a copy, gives a good indication of the state of my development at the time, as the following extract shows.

> *"He struck me as a very immature child indeed and for almost the whole of the verbal section of the test he was sucking his thumb. He was over friendly, making a very easy, but very shallow relationship and his behaviour was typical of that of a deprived child. I should judge him to have a lot of latent aggression. The development of his personality has by no means kept up with his intelligence and he has very little psychological stamina. In spite of his good intelligence he gives up very easily when faced with difficulty. I do not think he would fit very easily into a foster home."*

As I see it, there is a very clear correlation here to the minimal parental input for the first seven years of my life in terms of mental stimulation, and encouragement through games or other activities with them.

This state of my arrested development and inability to relate to adults or children on a satisfactory basis, is also borne out by my first school report there. In the section of general behaviour, the following was reported.

> *"Tony's general behaviour has been good, he has considerable ability and his work has been satisfactory, but he is inclined to be mentally lazy and lacks perseverance when faced with difficulty, the pattern of his behaviour at such a time, shows signs of immaturity for his age. Although accepted by other children, his relationship with them again shows signs of immaturity."*

So, as a result of these reports and a case conference held at the centre by the staff and someone from the Children's Department, it was decided that a possible admission to a long-term Children's Home called The Caldecott Community might be suitable for us.

In the interim life was pleasant enough, with a reassuring routine. On Saturday mornings we would go to the local cinema to see a western or some other children's film. Then on Sundays we either went to Church, or Sunday

School, and once a week we could go to the local shop to buy sweets. These were then stored in a tin (one for each child) and rationed out each night after meals and before going out to play.

The recreational facilities were quite good, with the fairly extensive grounds and a playroom, which had a good selection of toys and an old-fashioned wind-up gramophone on which to play 78 rpm records! This was dominated by two of the older girls, who tended to bully the younger children at times. One of them, had a terrible temper and would fight with the other girls. However, she was also quite good at drawing, and when she was sitting with her sketch book, she was very approachable and almost like a different person.

During our stay there, which lasted about six months we were visited fairly frequently by my mother, accompanied by Dennis, also by my father. These visits were marred a little by both of our parents trying hard to win our affections and, to some extent, influence us against the other parent.

An example of this can be found in the report on Colin on 1 January 1961 by the Warden.

"At first appeared normal well-behaved boy and did not appear at all unduly disturbed considering he had been

little with parents both of whom were suffering from mental instability. Deteriorated, particularly in the last three months. Has shown underlying anxiety and aggression. There are weekly visits from his parents on different days that have involved him in old family conflicts and each parent tried to "get at" the other one through the children. He has not been able to forget the violent disagreements between his parents. Can get nervously worked up and he has found it hard to live with uncertainty about his future. His irritation is sometimes vented on other people. Although Colin is fond of his mother, he has not found a group of women staff easy and he has lacked a good relationship with a man. Annoys and sometimes torments younger children, sometimes punching them or taking their sweets. Very occasional violent temper (deliberately broke window of his bedroom, will tear things up, stamp about swearing if very frustrated). Cannot bear to be thwarted, at times very resentful of authority and will deliberately disobey. Hoards things and keeps in secret places and resents any interference over this. Mean over spending, he very rarely buys sweets but is very fond of them and will try to persuade other children to give him theirs. Tries to bribe or barter to obtain other children's possessions. Bit of a lone wolf. Likes his own little corner and particularly a special locked place to keep his things in. Otherwise polite, well mannered, considerable creative faculty, much initiative, sense of responsibility, an underlying integrity and maturity beyond his years, a real sense of gratitude for what is done for him."

A highlight of our stay was when a few children were chosen to go on a trip to Dawlish, a seaside resort in Devon. We stayed at a boarding house and had a very enjoyable time playing in the sand on the beach and searching through rock pools for crabs or shrimps.

Back at the home, life continued as usual, until one day we were taken by our Child Care Officer on a long journey in his car, to be interviewed for a place at the Caldecott Community.

To say that I was overwhelmed by my first sight of the Caldecott Community, would be something of an understatement, for the building that it occupied was a stately home, designed by Robert Adam, called Mersham-le-Hatch. However, as the three of us walked up the front steps into the hall, although a little nervous, I did not feel intimidated.

We were interviewed by a Miss Dave, who was the deputy head. I don't remember any details of this, but afterwards we were shown around the magnificent house and introduced to the respective groups that Colin and I would each be placed in.

Unsurprisingly, I felt a little insecure at the thought of having to settle into yet another new environment and get to know the other children and staff. So, I felt a bit relieved when it was time to go back to the now familiar surroundings of the Assessment Centre. From there I was able over the next few weeks, to slowly adjust to the whole idea of moving again, which was a help. What is more, being December, we were taken to a local army camp, where a wonderful party was thrown for us, with all the sandwiches, cakes and jellies we could eat. There were games, a Christmas Tree and finally a Father Christmas who gave us all a present before we departed. All in all, our stay at the centre had been a very positive experience, which made life a little better for us.

So it was then, that on 10th January 1961, with me aged eight and Colin eleven, that we were brought to Caldecott to start our new life.

Chapter 10
Arrival at Caldecott

Mersham-le-Hatch was owned by Lord Brabourne and leased to the Caldecott Community at a very low rent. It is set in several hundred acres of land, including a wonderful Deer Park which spread out behind the magnificent mansion. The two lawns at the front of the building were flanked on either side by beautiful rhododendrons, which looked superb in full bloom in the spring. The extensive grounds were full of trees and shrubs and were a haven of peace.

Beyond the second lawn was a football pitch and a tennis court and adjacent to that was the cricket pitch. The football pitch was also used for exercising the ponies from the stables, and each year a Gymkhana was held there too. Children regularly went riding on the ponies supervised by a member of staff.

The buildings in the old stable yard had been adapted and were used as the nursery and primary schools. There was also a Chapel and a music room. Behind these was an extensive kitchen garden. Children from the age of eleven went out to the local Secondary and Grammar schools.

The interior of the building also warrants substantial description, with its huge Robert Adam doors and fireplaces and large sash windows, each one having its own individual view of the gorgeous surroundings. The entrance hall contained two very large solid oak tables, each capable of seating about sixteen people and next door to that was the very elegant dining room full of pictures of previous generations of the Brabourne family and a massive copy of a Canaletto painting of the Rialto Bridge in Venice.

The wooden floors were highly polished and there was a huge square stair well beyond the hall, which was made up of wrought ironwork with wooden bannisters.

Nearly all the staff at Caldecott in those days were elderly, but very dedicated women.

Upon our arrival at this incredible place, Colin and I were taken to our respective groups. The one that I had been assigned to was called the Junior Study and was made up of about twenty children, boys and girls, between the ages of six and eight years old. This group was situated on the top floor of the main house and was divided into three main areas. Firstly, there was the playroom, which was a big room at the back of the house that overlooked the

Deer Park. It had a large fireplace that always had a log fire blazing in it during the winter months and also a large wooden table at one end for playing games on. There were small chairs for us children and a couple of easy chairs for the adults. There were also several cupboards in the room, some of which contained toys and games and these were taken out at certain times of day, supervised by a member of staff.

The sleeping accommodation consisted of two dormitories, each with its own bathroom and lavatory, with one section for the girls and one for the boys. The number of boys and girls in the Junior Study were roughly equal and nearly all the activities that took place within the group involved them both. There were two members of staff allotted to looking after us, one for the boy's dormitory and one for the girls. One of them also took care of playroom activities.

Chapter 11
Life in the Junior Study

Upon my arrival in the Junior Study, I felt rather sad and bewildered as I saw my case being taken off to the dormitory for unpacking, until Miss Murdin, who ran the group, welcomed me and introduced me to another boy of my age. He befriended me, showed me the ropes and helped me to settle in. He had been at the Community for some while, having been in the nursery originally, and was very pleased to have recently been "promoted" to the Junior Study! I took an instant liking to this boy and we became firm friends, which continued throughout our time at the Community, and has continued to this day. I was most appreciative of his showing me the "ins and outs" of the place and explaining the rules.

Before long I began to feel more at ease and get to know both the place and the people and, although I didn't see much of Colin, I didn't mind too much, knowing all the time that he was at least around the place. As with the assessment centre, there was an ordered, calm existence and my thoughts and feelings were largely occupied with day to day life in my new environment and I was feeling reasonably happy.

The pattern of life consisted of rising at about 8am and having washed, dressed and cleaned our shoes, we would all proceed down the seven or eight flights of stairs, through the hall and into the dining room for breakfast. We would be joined at breakfast by the Senior Study, the next age group up, of which Colin was a member. The older Senior boys, eleven and upwards, would have already eaten and would be making their way to the bus stop to attend either the local Secondary Modern or Grammar schools.

Breakfast always followed the same pattern, which was Muesli on Mondays, ham on Tuesdays, eggs on Wednesdays, porridge on Thursdays and cereal on Fridays. On weekends it was kippers and haddock. These were accompanied by toast, or rolls and butter, with marmalade. There was also an item known as "Scrunch". This was really just plain bread, which was a day or two old, and had been baked in the oven to make it crunchy! We also had Camp coffee served in large blue mugs from a huge metal urn.

When breakfast was over, we would make our way back upstairs to the playroom for a short period before going over to school. Classes were split into three age groups. Our class was run by a woman who was fairly plump, had a bad hip, and a rather red face. She was always kind, but could keep very firm control of the class, when needed. She also had a delightful little beagle dog called "Topsy" who was a great joy to us children.

The schoolwork here was always interesting and fun. I remember doing drawings and paintings and making papier mache puppets, by pasting old newspapers onto a plasticine model. We also once all saved the cream from our break-time milk and made it into butter and then had a little on our bread at teatime that evening.

Once a week, we were required to write to our parents or relatives. I always found it rather a tiresome task as apart from a few details about what we had been doing, I could think of very little else to say.

The schoolwork was punctuated by a short break in the mornings and afternoons, during which, in the morning, a small bottle of milk and two sweet biscuits were eagerly consumed. We then indulged in the usual playground games of "Tag" and "Hide and Seek" and so on. We also used to climb the big beech tree and swing on a rope that was tied to one of the branches, whilst the girls would sit on the grass in summer and make daisy chains. They also enjoyed playing hopscotch by the garages.

We must have done Maths, English and Geography in some form, but I don't recall much about them in the early days. I think these were more likely to have been done in more detail in the other two classes as we got older.

We did learn about the Romans, though, which I found interesting. However, the highlight for me was the last half hour of school each day when Mrs Robson would read books to us, such as Mary Poppins and Worzel Gummidge. She was a very good reader and always tailored her voice to suit the different characters. She also read us "The Hobbit" and "The Lord of the Rings", which I found absolutely enthralling.

At lunchtime, we would go to the main house, back to our playroom and wash our hands. Life at Caldecott was to some extent governed by bells being rung certain times of day, whereupon certain actions had to be taken. One of these was for mealtimes, so when the outside bell rang, we once again descended the stairs and took our places in the dining room.

The food at Caldecott was very good on the whole, considering that it was an institution that had to cater to over 100 children in those days. Many of the vegetables were grown in the huge kitchen garden of the stately home and were really good and also very fresh. My favourite meals at lunchtime were steak and kidney pie, although I now no longer eat meat, with two veg, one of which in the summer was very often lovely new potatoes, which had been dug up that morning. There were always plenty of these and if one table had finished theirs and wanted more, the bowl could be taken around other tables, to see if they had any spare. I used to love eating rice pudding too, which was quite stodgy and very filling.

Meals were mostly carried out in two sittings, namely the seniors followed by the juniors, mainly for reasons of space. These meals were always conducted by Miss Leila, who controlled each stage of the meal by the tinkling of a little hand bell. This would signal a period of silence before either clearing the tables between courses or dismissing each table at the end of a meal. If a child was late for a meal, they would be expected to stand for a few minutes behind their chair, before being allowed to sit down and eat their food. Similarly, any child who was rude at the table or showed bad manners, would also have to stand behind their chair and remain silent for a short time as a punishment for their rudeness.

After lunch we would go into the very impressive library for what was known simply, as 'rest'. This meant taking a tartan rug from one of the cupboards, laying down on it on the floor and reading a book for half an hour. These books were taken from the local library and there was a woman who very helpfully guided us as to the sort of books she felt that we might like. I remember reading an assortment of books in my early years ranging from Biggles, to a series of adventure books about twins from different countries, through to Enid Blyton's "Secret Seven" and "Five" books.

After rest, we would wander back over to the schoolyard for our afternoon lessons, which ended about 4pm. An afternoon activity, amongst other things in Mrs Robson's class, was doing a little bit of gardening. Each child had a tiny plot in which to grow various vegetables or flowers.

Mrs Robson, very sadly, was a widow, because of her husband dying of pulmonary tuberculosis right at the end of WW2. He had been a stretcher bearer. Apparently, he used to write to her regularly of his experiences. She decided to write a book containing his letters and it was published in his name in 1961. It is called "Letters from a Soldier" by Walter Robson and was very well received by the critics.

After school, we would go back to the house for high tea, which would be our last meal of the day. On Thursdays, this meal had the added treat of being followed by an ice cream. We would then go to the playroom for a short while before bedtime, which was around 6:30pm. Once in bed, we had about half an hour in which to read, update stamp albums, or do other similar activities.

Then Miss Murdin would read to us from various books for 15 minutes or so, before lights out. I recall "Treasure Island", "Coral Island" and stories by E. Nesbit, such as "5 Children and It", "The Phoenix and the Carpet" and "The Story of the Amulet".

On Saturday mornings we attended the school on the premises until midday and these few hours were usually taken up with woodwork or arts and crafts. As for the rest of the weekend, that consisted of games in the grounds and fairly long walks with a group of us children going along country lanes being led by Miss Murdin. To any bemused person passing by she must have looked like a "Mother Hen" leading all her "Chicks" behind her! At the end of it, we would spend our pocket money in the local sweetshop.

This cycle of life continued for me in the Junior Study for about six months, which passed, on the whole, fairly happily. During this period, Colin and I were visited once or twice by my mother who was now living in a bed sitting room and working as a typist. She would hire a car for a day or weekend and travel with Dennis to come and see us. These visits from mother and Dennis were fairly frequent, usually about twice a term on average, and they continued throughout the eight years that I was at the community, although at a slightly scaled-down rate.

My father, however, whilst quite keen to see us in our new surroundings initially, was totally averse to driving long distances. This was largely, I suppose, because he felt unfit or unable to drive other than for short journeys, because of the medications he was taking for his mental and emotional condition. On the occasions he did come down, he hired somebody to drive the car for him. As such, he only visited us two or three times at Caldecott altogether. We did visit both of our parents during the school holidays, though.

Any visits made by either parent were always greatly looked forward to by Colin and me and when, on one or two occasions, a visit was postponed for one reason or another, bitter disappointment and a feeling of rejection would set in and would take several days to shake off. This was regardless of what the reason was, even if we knew that it could not be helped.

However, these visits, when they did take place, were always very enjoyable and usually consisted of trips to various seaside towns nearby and included picnics on the beach and walks and ice creams.

Money, as far as my mother was concerned, was still very tight and I often felt a mixture of anger and sorrow when she explained that she could not afford to let us have more than one turn on the dodgems, or a few pennies for the slot machines, because of this. The anger was not directed at her, but more at a set of circumstances that could allow a situation like this to exist. The sorrow I felt, though, was more for her, knowing that she really wanted to provide for us, not just materially, but in every other way too, and was unable to do so.

These aspects aside however, visits were by and large very happy affairs and always as the day wore on, with the time of their departure growing ever more imminent, a feeling of sadness would slowly creep over me. It was always with a lump in my throat and a forced smile that we kissed and waved mother and Dennis goodbye and watched them drive off, until the car was completely out of sight. After a day or so, the sadness would wear off and normal life would resume, and I would focus my thoughts in other areas.

In November of that year, my ninth birthday arrived, and there was always a great deal of importance attached to birthdays at the community. Firstly, there was a specially made oak noticeboard, which hung in the hall and each month all the children who had a birthday would have their name written in italics on a card, with the date and inserted into a slot on the board for all to see. On the top half of the board there was a picture, which changed each month as well, like an ordinary calendar. Having one's name put up in this way always made one feel very special and full of pleasant anticipation. On the day itself, the member of staff responsible would give the child in question a little present which they had specially bought on their day off. In addition to this, a birthday party was given in the dining room, with a cake and candles. This party was combined with high tea, and the person whose birthday it was, could choose who would sit at their table.

At the end of Colin's and my first term, the holidays duly arrived.

Chapter 12
Holidays

At that time in its history Caldecott was only open during the term time. So, for the holidays, the children either went home to their parents, if possible, or to holiday foster homes, or anywhere that could be found for them. Colin and I ended up going back to the Reception Assessment Centre for the Easter holidays. This went off well enough, except that Colin had a bitter row with our mother, which went on for some considerable time before reconciliation took place.

However, by the time the summer holidays arrived the Children's Department had found a foster home for us, at least for a part of that holiday. The rest of it was spent on a farm in Suffolk, which belonged to the parents of a member of staff at Caldecott. The holiday with the foster parents was only intended as a temporary arrangement to begin with, but it soon became more permanent.

Our new foster parents were a couple in their early thirties. John was a Curate and his wife Margaret had been a teacher, who, we discovered later, had sometimes taught my eldest brother, Dennis, when we lived on the farm. They had two children of their own and another one on the way.

Colin and I arrived in July 1961 to be given a cheery welcome from Margaret, who was heavily pregnant at the time, and were shown to our own room in the small, but pleasant house provided by the Church.

Right from the start Margaret tried to engage us in things to do and suggested fairly early on, that we might like to decorate our own room with wallpaper of our own choosing. We thus had a rather adventurous, if not slightly messy time, papering the walls and painting the woodwork. I think we actually did quite a reasonable job given our ages, and the fact that we had never done any decorating before! She also encouraged us to take up a hobby and we bought and put together Airfix kits of model aeroplanes, which we then suspended from the ceiling with pieces of cotton. They were all put at different angles, so as to represent a still-life dog fight in the sky, as it were.

Our first Christmas holiday there was magical. When we first arrived there was a small Christmas tree in the sitting room, surrounded by lots of presents and we used to love to pore over them and identify those which were for us and try to guess what was in them. This gave us several days of pleasurable anticipation before Christmas Day and really helped to get us in the mood. On the day itself, having hung up our large stockings alongside those of John and Margaret's children on Christmas Eve, we would wake up to find them on the end of our beds in the morning.

These stockings had our own names on them and were jampacked with good size presents, all in addition to those around the Christmas tree and what's more, each one was individually wrapped in Christmas paper.

Having opened the stockings, we would then have breakfast with the other members of the family and discuss what we had each received. We then got dressed and went off to attend the church at which John was the Curate and returned afterwards to have a lunch of tea and sandwiches.

After lunch, would come the present giving proper, the highlight of the day and at this stage we could hardly contain our excitement. The presents would be handed out by John, one at a time, and this whole operation would last a good hour or more. Then we would all play with our respective toys and gifts until about 6 o'clock in the evening, when we would have the Christmas dinner. This was always a huge affair with plenty of food and John, when we were a bit older, would even allow Colin and me a little wine to go with our meal. This all really seemed to sum up the true Spirit of Christmas.

The following poem, I hope, captures the essence of this.

Christmas Lights.

We love the lights of Christmas,
they sparkle and they glow.
They lift the hearts of shoppers
and brighten up a show.

What joy to hear the carols
and all the Christmas songs.
To share with all our families
and know that we belong.

We love to open presents
to see just what's inside.
And see the joy of loved ones;
our warmth we cannot hide.

We spare a thought for lonely ones,
the homeless and the old.
We need to share our warmth with them,
not leave them in the cold.

When midnight chimes on Christmas Eve,
Church windows are ablaze,
as Christians go to worship God
and joyfully sing his praise.

We love the lights of Christmas,
the birth of Christ our Lord.
He lights our hearts forever,
eternity assured.

Our main contact for most of the years that we spent with our foster parents was with Margaret, as John had many parish duties to perform, so was less available. He was very conscientious with his work and at one time a pregnant "unmarried mother", as they were referred to in those days, stayed briefly in the house with us. Margaret and John were clearly giving her some support, although I had no idea of any details of her circumstances. One thing I remember about her, though, was that when she laughed, she would snort along with it which Colin and I found terribly funny! Sometimes her boyfriend would drop by for a visit and seemed to take a shine to us. He would sometimes have play fights with us and we got on well with him.

One of the joys of the household were the two mongrel dogs, one of whom was slightly lame and was sadly put to sleep quite soon after our second holiday with them.

The other, however, lived for a good many years and we both doted on this dog who was like a small St. Bernard.

Despite the fact that we much enjoyed being with our foster parents and grew very fond of them, it was not long before problems began to emerge, for a number of reasons.

In the first place, we found it rather difficult to relate to them and their children in a way that they would have liked. I think they didn't quite realise what they were taking on with two young children from a broken home and maybe had unrealistic expectations of us. Clearly, they were both well motivated in taking us on and trying to provide a loving and nurturing environment for us. However, they found for much of the time our lack of emotional response and general inability to interact with their family, increasingly frustrating over the years.

I know that both Colin and I were suffering from varying degrees of emotional trauma, due to the experiences we had been through during our early years. Speaking for myself, I was incredibly withdrawn, so much so, that I didn't always hear when people spoke to me. This had nothing to do with my physical hearing, which was perfectly normal, but what I can only conclude was a defence mechanism from all the shouting and rows of parents and the ensuing upheaval. It was safer to simply withdraw into my own world. However, by so doing, I substantially placed myself out of reach of others.

The following extract from our files highlights this.

> Margaret was concerned about Tony who often appeared not to hear what was being said to him. She had the impression that his thoughts were far away, even Colin had noticed this and had said he is going daft. Moreover, Tony grunts ("a sigh with a grunt at the end") persistently. Even when eating, he is completely unconscious of this and that it is aggravating to others. Neither of them are interested in reading, only in television in the evenings and model plane making during the day."

Margaret, after a while, grew rather impatient with my apparent deafness and used to taunt me from time to time, which I found rather hurtful. I believe that to some extent both Colin and I were not really capable of understanding the basic mechanics of human interaction, and so were unable to contribute significantly, in any meaningful way to foster family life. This bears out the Psychologist's report on me at the reception assessment centre, when he thought that I would not fit very easily into a foster home.

Given that human relationships are so very important then my lack of ability to perform adequately within them, was not only my loss, but was also to the hurt and detriment of those around me. This was made apparent, initially at the foster parents' home, but was also true throughout the whole of my time in local authority care and beyond. However, this was not something that I realised till very many years later.

Another significant problem that arose was the fact that we were only with Margaret and John during the holidays, as the term times were spent at Caldecott. This meant that access to our parents for visits was rather restricted in term time due to the distances our parents each individually had to travel to come and see us.

So, the holidays for both parents were a crucial time to see more of us because of the relative proximity to each of them from our foster home. Unfortunately, this meant that Margaret and John found the pressures of our family visits became a strain on them, sometimes because of the unreasonable demands of our parents, particularly our mother, and also the effect the visits had on us.

This state of affairs led to considerable wrangling between the foster parents, our own parents and the local authority children's department, as they tried to sort out visiting arrangements that would suit all parties. It was decided that seeing our parents during the holidays should be cut down as a result. This evoked some bitterness and hurtful reactions, which did not make for harmonious or constructive relationships all round. This situation rumbled along in the background in varying degrees for virtually all the years that we were with Margaret and John.

So, our first three holidays with Margaret and John went well on the whole, but by the summer of 62 things took a rather different turn as the files indicate.

> *"28 September 1962. Notes of Mr M (Child Care Officer) visit to foster parents. Unwilling to have Colin again. Isle of Wight farm holiday not a success. Dissension all the time. Neither of us showed initiative, just hung around waiting for foster parents' suggestions. Colin unwilling to carry anything, gave his knapsack to Tony to carry. Only did what he wanted to do, such as cooking (which he was quite good at). Become a most unpleasant character. Adverse effect on eldest son. Unmerciful bullying, physical and mental, of Tony (also bullying eldest son to lesser extent). Thinks he is always right, Tony never. Eldest son copies Colin and has become quite unbearable since Colin's return to Caldecott. Tony remembers people, Colin only things. Materialistic to an extreme, thinking only of money and what he can get out of people. Grown-up in handling money, not wasting a penny. On foster mothers' birthday (which the boys knew nothing about until the morning), they went into the local town, but instead*

of buying her some little thing, they spent their money on themselves except that Tony did buy a birthday card which he gave to foster mother. Colin, however, excused himself by saying he had not had enough money left over to buy her anything! Expect the best for himself always, resent Tony (in particular) receiving anything, however small. He encouraged Tony to use up his free film quickly, taking ridiculous pictures, so that he would receive his free film more quickly. He calls the dog away from Tony so he can say the dog loves him more, Tony loves the dog but for him just a means of getting at Tony, (this was not entirely true, as he did love the dog too). *The parents, of course, are at the root of the trouble. Foster mother thinks that Mrs Inwood gives Colin the impression that she is the injured party and the foster parents feel that he has probably more feeling for her than for his father. At the same time, he is friendly with his father, at least partly no doubt, for what he can get out of him. In fact, Mr Inwood gives much to Colin, but very little to Tony, merely calling him his little sweetheart and darling! Presumably Mr Inwood is attempting to "buy" Colin from Mrs Inwood. Tony and Colin have nothing in common and meet only in the holidays. There are no boys of Colin's age near the foster home and the foster parents think that he would be more at home among boys older or about the same age as himself. They also think that Tony would be better away from Colin. Tony on his own is not a problem as they say he can be found things to do which he will*

*enjoy. The foster parents are willing to keep Tony but
not Colin, chiefly because of his influence on eldest son."*

As a result of this there began the on/off possibility that
I might live with them permanently and go to a local
school. However, as this further extract shows, the
situation with parental visits was soon resolved.

*"15 October 1962. Notes by Miss Dave (Deputy head of
Caldecott) of a report by Mr M (Child Care Officer – CCO)
to her of a conversation with Colin over lunch in Ashford.
A very satisfactory talk with Colin. He felt Colin had
matured and for the first time he was able to talk about the
family problems objectively. Colin had written an apology
to the foster parents for his behaviour in the holidays and
had prepared a parcel containing a small present for the
eldest son's birthday.*

*Mr M's own report of his visit to Caldecott and of
the Ashford conversation with Colin (and a separate
conversation with Tony). A C.C.O. from Kent had also
attended this meeting with Miss Dave and the C.C.O.
had prepared notes of that meeting. After that meeting
Mr M had a conversation with Tony and then, with Tony,
collected Colin from the North Modern school, to go into
Ashford for lunch. Colin chatted easily to Mr M, but Tony
seemed more intent on his lunch than mere talk. Mr M
had earlier questioned Tony closely (privately) about*

his relationship with Colin and there is no doubt that Tony is fond of his brother and he is most definite about not wanting to spend a holiday apart from him. Tony is enthusiastic about staying with the foster parents and, although he quite likes Caldecott, he is looking forward to the day when, like Colin, he can attend school in Ashford. After lunch Mr M put Tony on a bus back to Caldecott before talking privately with Colin. Mr M feels he can now talk very directly to Colin without his appearing to resent it. Colin admitted at once that his behaviour had been poor but said in part explanation that he had been worried about his mother, who had told him in confidence, that she was having to leave her employment. Mr M said he appreciated that but then listed the various bad behaviours the foster parents had explained to him (as per the notes higher up). Colin seemed genuinely sorry and assured him that he would try to do better. He had bought presents for the two older children. Miss Dave had told him that these presents had been bought <u>before</u> he had been told of the foster parents' complaints about his behaviour and that the letter of apology followed Miss Dave talking to him (he had enclosed the letter in the parcel, which he gave to Mr M and asked him to give to the foster parents). He was adamant that he would not want to spend a holiday away from Tony. Although they see little of each other at Caldecott, Mr M thinks that he is happy to know that Tony is not far away. Colin had said to Mr M that he hoped he would be going to the foster *parents in future. Mr M said that he would be talking to the foster parents and that Colin would hear from Miss Dave whether or not Tony and he would be spending Christmas with them."*

So, the situation was patched up, but only temporarily.

Chapter 13
The Senior Study

When I was 9 years old, I was transferred to a new group called the Senior Study. Life here was much the same as in the Junior Study with one or two exceptions. At that age we were considered old enough to do a small job of housework after breakfast each day.

Schoolwork also became a little bit more sophisticated. In addition to the basic subjects, we did various projects connected with television programmes relating to geography and biology, for example. I did a project on how the human body works and I still have it as a valued part of my personal possessions today. We also did field trips to places of interest locally, like a bakery, a brickworks and various others.

The music room run by a Miss Betty Rayment and we did singing in her classes. She would also play short extracts of classical music, which generated an interest in the subject for me, and I'm sure for others, which developed in later life. Some of the children were gifted in playing musical instruments too, such as the violin or piano and Miss Rayment was very good at encouraging them through one to one lessons and one boy went on to become a concert pianist.

There were a whole range of general activities throughout the year, which were highlights and much enjoyed by all. There was a Gymkhana in the summer months as well as camping trips. A Sports Day for the Junior school, with a slap-up tea for all afterwards. Then in the autumn and winter months, Fancy Dress and Talent Nights, Scottish dancing, and a special party to celebrate Miss Leila's birthday in October.

The Junior School also took part in an activity called eurhythmics. This was held in the library and basically involved dancing around to music and sliding along wooden floorboards. This often resulted in getting splinters in rather uncomfortable places!

On Sundays we were obliged to attend a small Chapel on the premises, except for Catholics, who went instead to a nearby Catholic Church. The service was taken by Leila Rendel, the head of Caldecott, who was a committed Quaker. It was a mixture of Anglicanism and Quakerism. Apparently, the local Vicar used to refer to it affectionately as "Rendelianism"!

Apart from hymns, there were also assorted talks by various members of staff, including Leila herself, who did a whole series on building the "Bricks" of the human character. These talks on the whole, were more of a general ethical nature than necessarily relating to the Christian faith directly.

An important milestone at the beginning and end of every term was the school meeting. It was a very well organised affair and had to be rehearsed in detail by the Junior School, two or three days before it was due to take place. This ceremony had something in the nature of a "Trooping of the Colour" air about it and was conducted with great reverence.

It always took place in the library, which was a substantial room and capable when full, of holding all the school pupils without it being too cramped. All the furniture was neatly arranged, with the mock Chippendale table being brought in from the hall and placed squarely in front of the mantelpiece, with two chairs tucked in behind it. It was in these chairs that Miss Leila and Miss Dave would sit, regally surveying the rest of the library.

Either side of this table there were two more chairs which were for the two Heralds. These Heralds were usually both prefects (PPU's) and there was normally one boy and one girl. Opposite them, at the back of the library, was a long row of chairs which seated the remaining prefects, in addition to nearly all the members of staff, as this ceremony included the whole school except for the nursery children.

Then, in front of these chairs, there would stand rows of children in order of age, with the oldest ones at the back. The children were grouped into two halves, with the girls on one side, and the boys on the other. In order for the children to get into these positions, they had to march in row by row from the doors at either end of the library. This marching took place to the accompaniment of "The Washington Post" by John Paul Sousa. This was suitably stirring March music and was played with great gusto on the piano, by Miss Rayment, the music teacher.

Gradually, each row would file in, age group by age group until we would all be present and correct and standing with our hands clasped in front of us. Whilst waiting to come in, children would start marching on the spot to the music to ensure their entrance ran smoothly. However, on one occasion, one of the boys in front, decided to change feet which threw the marching into confusion and caused a bit of a shambles!

There was a strict dress code for this occasion, namely, uniforms. For the younger boys this consisted of grey shorts, white shirts and a blue tie. The older boys wore grey shorts, blue shirts and grey jerseys, which all looked very drab. The girls wore an equally drab uniform as well!

Once all were neatly assembled, Miss Leila would tell us to sit. The over 14 age group had chairs provided, but because of lack of space, the younger age groups sat on the floor. When everyone was duly seated, the "Charter" would be respectfully read out by both Miss Leila and the two Heralds, who each had their own section to read.

After the charter was finished, Miss Leila and the two Heralds would sit down and hand over the proceedings to Miss Dave, who after a brief pause, would stand up and regale us with news of various children who had left. These she had either seen during the holidays, or they had written to her during the term. Most were good news stories of the life they were carving out for themselves, but some were rather sad tales of those who had ended up in rather sorry situations.

Next, would come reports of how children had done in their respective exams. This was always carried out with a slight air of the pep talk about it, in order to try and encourage all the children to work hard and achieve excellence in all things, as well as praising those who had achieved good results.

After this, at the end of term meetings, came the housework reports. Housework was carried out by all the children over the age of nine, in addition to some of the staff. However, the latter, did not, of course, feature in such reports! These tasks were by no means arduous and served a dual purpose. This being to give practical assistance to the staff in maintaining a good standard of cleanliness and also to make each child aware of the importance of a clean and tidy environment. Housework was always treated with mixed feelings among the children, and the reports fully reflected this!

Each was written by the member of staff to whom the child had been assigned and was intended as a measure of either praise or rebuff, according to the performance given. In addition to this, a housework present was always kindly given at the end of term to each child, regardless of whether it was a good performance or not. Some children, me included, did not really take to housework. So occasionally the reports when judiciously read out by Miss Dave reflected this and would give rise to hoots of laughter from the assembled children, when a particularly unfortunate comment was made about a child's conduct! This laughter was sometimes frowned upon by Miss Dave, who on occasions, would rebuke us in the most serious of tones saying that it "was not really a laughing matter".

Meeting would then end with a song, which was either "Jerusalem" or "Non Nobis Domine". This would be sung lustily by one and all and then after a prayer, we would all march out to the same stirring music that we had come in on.

Although this meeting was a very worthwhile affair, some of us found it rather quaint and even giggled afterwards about some aspects of it that struck us as funny. Similarly, the Charter, although not necessarily appreciated by all at the time, was a very valuable document and contains extremely wise words. I include the text below.

The Charter of the Caldecott Community

This household is a community. The members of this community are the boys and girls and grown-up people. In connection with these are the parents and many friends who help us with their good will and their money.

Every group of people living together is a community. The first group is a family. Life in a family prepares us for life in a school. Life in a school prepares us for a life of work in the world, or as part of another household.

All these communities have their own rules and laws, and each community has to obey the law of the country in which it exists. Laws of conduct and health which the wisdom of their chosen leaders has decided to make.

Such laws are worth keeping because the obedience of each helps the happiness of all, where many live together.

Willingness to submit to laws is the payment made for that order and comfort which such laws maintain. Such laws can only govern and maintain a community so long as they are accepted with humility, followed with faithfulness and maintained with justice.

1st Herald.

The members of this community shall live together with honour and loyalty, that is: They shall speak the truth, respect other people's property and never steal. They shall be prepared to serve the community – by observing the common courtesies of life, by obeying the bye laws of the community, made for the convenience and safety of the household, by being careful and helpful with those younger

than themselves, kindly and just to their equals, generous minded and considerate towards their elders.

2nd Herald.

By learning to be wise and controlled in the care of their own bodies and minds. By facing difficulties courageously, rising after defeat and being humble in the face of success.

The acceptance of these laws fits the members of the community to render faithful service in the future to the land to which they belong and to contribute what lies in their power to the happiness and welfare of men and women of any race.

Above all, remembering that the community exists in common with all mankind, solely that it may go forward on an eternal quest, forever seeking to discover God's purpose for his world and for each individual soul in his world.

Of all the activities that took place each year, I think, for me, the best of all was Christmas. What a joy that was. There would be a Christmas party with exciting games in the library, followed by some fabulous food in the dining room. Then we would all file into one of the large rooms between the dining room and the library and sit down in front of a huge Christmas tree, which was beautifully adorned and with masses of present scattered beneath it. A few carols would then be sung, which all helped to create the special magical atmosphere.

Then came the present giving. As each present was handed out by Miss Dave, the eager anticipation grew, as each child awaited theirs. The staff took a great deal of trouble to buy presents that they knew would interest each child – no mean feat, when each group they bought for could be between 15 to 20 children.

The other important aspect of Christmas was the Chapel Service, with the Christmas story being told by Miss Leila, assisted by two senior girls. This was punctuated by the wonderful carols, which were sung using a special home-made book of Carols.

My time in the Senior Study was relatively short, however, as in early 1963 I was transferred to a smaller group called The Paddocks. This was based in a house a few miles away from Hatch and was run by James and Tessa King. It was created to have more of a family atmosphere about it, albeit a rather large one and it was felt that I would benefit more from being there.

Chapter 14
The Paddocks

The Paddocks was a rambling Victorian Manor House, set in fairly extensive grounds with two lawns bedecked on either side by Rhododendrons, in a pattern similar to those at Hatch, but smaller. It had a tennis court, a little copse of trees, and a miniature "swimming pool" called the Duck Pond. It housed about 20 children, both boys and girls aged between 7 and 14. It had a huge, studded oak front door and a highly patterned mosaic tiled floor in the entrance hall. The gravel drive in front had a small circle of grass in the middle of it and two large oak gates, which always stood open.

My Junior Study friend had recently gone there and was so enamoured with the place that he suggested I might like to go as well. So, he asked James King (affectionately known as "Bingy") if I could transfer there too. This was then duly arranged.

I already knew the other children there, as Paddocks life was integrated into Hatch in various ways, such as school attendance, some meals and Chapel. It was also within easy walking distance so very convenient. Thus, happily, settling in was not a problem.

Fairly soon after I moved in, a new boy came to stay at the Paddocks who then shared a bedroom with me and my Junior study friend. After a very short space of time the three of us became very good friends and formed a trio which lasted throughout the whole of our time at the community.

Life was good at the Paddocks with lots of interesting things to do. We had a "Dirt Track", which was for riding bikes and went through trees and up and down small inclines and so on. We had a super time riding round it and it was good exercise too! We were also given the freedom to cycle around the local area. We couldn't afford to buy bikes, of course, so we had to make up our own from frames, handlebars and wheels etc., that were kept in the old workshop. Some of these parts were kindly given to us by a man called Skip Hudson who ran a bicycle shop in nearby Ashford. Simon Rodway, a member of staff at Caldecott who ran a section for older boys called the Colt House, had befriended him some years earlier when he used to go on cycle rides with the older boys. So, Skip was very happy to help out a local Children's home. We also used to visit the local dump (waste re-cycling site in modern speak) and found useful additions to our home-made bikes there.

The most important room at the Paddocks was a big playroom at the back of the house, which overlooked the lawns. We had a small snooker table in there which was well used and we had a "Snooker Ladder", which was a kind of league table for challenge matches. We also played billiards, as well as a great game called "Slosh". This was easy to play and meant one could rack up really high scores, especially good, if one wasn't very handy with the cue! Most satisfying! Card games also featured a lot and there was a very raucous one called "Pit". This was a market trading game with farmers selling wheat, oats and barley, as well as farm animals too. I don't recall exactly how it worked, but it was a fabulous game.

On the lawn outside, we would often play a game called "Tin Can Tommy". This was a group game consisting of one person in the middle of the lawn by an old tin can and holding a large stick. He or she was supposed to search out people hiding in the bushes. If they spotted one, they had to run back to the tin can, tap it with the stick, whilst announcing the name of the hideaway person, who was then out of the game. If they managed to find them all they had won. However, during searching they had to watch out that somebody didn't run out un-noticed and kick the tin over. In that event the game was then lost to the searcher! This was a wonderful way to while away an hour or so! We also played Tennis and enjoyed this summer activity a great deal, especially during all the excitement of Wimbledon.

Other memories of the gardens were James King mowing the lawns and the wonderfully evocative smell of grass cuttings mixed with petrol where the lawn mower was stored. Also, the amazing tree camp built by several of us and the ingenious aerial runway (Zip Wire), that ran from it down to the ground.

On Sunday afternoons we would have "Skippy" chocolate bars for tea and then listen to "Pick of the Pops" with Alan Freeman on the big old "Wireless" (Radio) in the playroom. Later on, we took it in turns to do "Cooking", which was supervised by Tessa. This was open to boys and girls and we used to cook delicious fudge or cheese straws in large quantities on the old Aga. This was then ceremoniously shared out on Sunday evenings at the traditional "Reading", where a member of staff would read to us all for half an hour or so before we took off to bed. It was all a very cosy affair and the perfect way to round off the weekend.

There were, of course, occasions when there was friction between some of us children and James King, usually over small items of discipline. I have to say that he always handled them firmly, but with kindness and patience. In my case, other issues took place, which I can only describe as rows or intense emotional outbursts, which he dealt with in the same way.

Two very significant things happened to me at this time. The first was my growing awareness of the lack of physical affection and however good the standard of care was at the Paddocks; physical affection was not a part of it. This was probably for very good reasons, after all how could a small number of staff provide proper emotional warmth and physical affection for upwards of 20 children. I suppose that up until that point I had been repressing that need and it was only now during this period of stability and feeling more secure that it rose to the surface. This became an ongoing problem throughout the whole of my childhood and even into early adulthood. So apart from the very early days of sitting on my dad's knee, this was punctuated, very briefly, on only a handful of occasions.

James and Tessa had two children of their own and the family had a small part of the house that were their private quarters, although on occasions they would invite us in spontaneously, to listen to records or just chat. However, for much of the time their children were a part of the Paddocks community and joined in with meals and general activities.

Their children, each had a bedside lamp in their rooms and I became a little jealous of this because we were not allowed them. I would complain about this to James from time to time and on one occasion, it blew up into a major row and I became more and more angry and hysterical.

James tried patiently to explain to me, that although part of the overall Paddocks family, they were his own children and because of that, were in that sense treated differently.

I could not accept this and after this row had dragged on for some considerable time, James could see that he was not making any real headway with me and left me on my own for a bit, to cool down. Then later Tessa came in, sat down next to me and put her arm around my shoulder and told me that they loved me and offered some other words of comfort that I cannot now recall.

It occurs to me that they may have realised that there was a limit to the kind of care they could provide for us all and perhaps, ideally, would have liked it to be more. Nonetheless, what they were able to give was of tremendous value and I shall always be very grateful for it.

My complaints about the table lamps (unjustified on my part, but understandable), were not, in fact, about table lamps at all. What I wanted on one level, I suppose, was an unrealistic kind of inclusion into their family unit, but far more powerfully, I was subconsciously crying out for physical warmth and affection. I now regard the lack of this as the most destructive force in my early life. In fact, I consider that I would not have developed my later feelings of depression and negativity to anywhere near the same extent, as the subsequent bad experiences occurred in my life, had this been forthcoming.

Another occasion concerned my foster mother, Margaret. She was very good with her own children, having fun and showing affection, physical and otherwise. However, Colin and I did not get any. Strangely, it did not seem odd to me in the early days there, but really just seemed "normal". It was only at the Paddocks when I did begin to feel it and badly. To be fair to Margaret, she did explain to us some years later that she felt she and John could not fully play a parental role in our lives, as our own parents were still alive and involved with us. It wasn't as if they had adopted us, which would have been different. I don't know if that was a right decision or not.

Nonetheless, there was one exception to this. My foster father's Church was "High Church" and there was quite a lot of incense during the service. One day I was overpowered by it and fainted. The next thing I knew was that I was sitting in the Church porch with someone waving smelling salts under my nose. To my surprise, Margaret was sitting next to me, with her arm around me and as I recovered, I leant against her briefly and remember just how good that felt.

The second thing of significance, is that in September 1964, having failed my 11 plus exam, I started to attend the local secondary modern school nearby. This proved to be a very difficult step for me. Having spent the previous three years or so of my life in a rather cocooned environment, the harsh reality of an ordinary school, with other children and masters, who were not aware of my personal background, made me feel very anxious and insecure. Coupled with this was the fact that my brother, Colin, who had already started at this school, had since been transferred to another secondary school some 10 miles away. So even though I had all my friends from Caldecott around me, I would very much have liked to see Colin around as well.

The school which Colin now attended was actually a very good secondary modern, but with an emphasis on agriculture and horticulture and had a small farm on the premises. Colin attended this school, because he felt at that time that he wanted to follow in our father's footsteps and become a farmer. Fortunately for me, James King, who was aware of my difficulties, arranged for me to be transferred to this school as well, after just a few weeks. I was very glad about this, knowing that Colin was also at that school.

Nonetheless, it did not allay all my insecurities and anxieties. For here, apart from Colin and one other boy from the Paddocks, there were no Caldecott friends around me. Thus, I was rather fearful in the early stages of attending yet another new school. This, after all, was the 8th school that I had attended, 6 of which had been primary.

James King had also arranged for me to have a brand-new satchel to take with me to this school, which, strangely, I drew much comfort from as a form of security, for it was a part of James King and the Paddocks that I could have with me. It became a kind of friend for me. So much so, that I would talk to it, not out loud, but in my mind, and this strange ritual got me through the first few weeks in what for me was a very threatening new environment.

After two or three months my anxieties grew less as I became familiar with my surroundings, the teachers, and made some friends. This included a group of boys who came from a village nearby and caught the same bus as me, both to and from school. This then became an added pleasure, as I always enjoyed their company and vicariously lapped up the tales of their evening activities. I never actually took part in them, though, as my spare time was always spent at the Paddocks.

At around this period, my father for some reason switched more of his affections to Colin and I began to feel resentful towards him and did not really want to write to him. As a result, my father wrote to Miss Dave at Caldecott asking why I had not sent him any letters. She wrote back saying merely that if I did not wish to write there was no point whatever in forcing me to do so, as in all probability any letter that I did write would not be worth receiving.

This resentment towards my father grew slowly over a period of two or three years and I occasionally felt rather hurt by his rejection of me in favour of Colin.

A year or so before I went out to school, our Child Care Officer (CCO) left the department and was replaced by another man. This was the first of several changes of CCO's that we were to experience whilst we were in care. This second man remained with us for 18 months or so before moving on himself, only to leave a gap which could not immediately be filled. Between then and the age of 18, I had two more childcare officers, each with gaps in between, filled by somebody else temporarily. These changes of CCO proved to be a rather unsettling experience because of having to keep making new relationships.

In March 1965, my mother's divorce was granted to her after six years of having left my father. As a result, a decision had to be made as to which parent would be given custody of us children, both Colin and I had to speak to a Judge in private to answer certain questions. I do not remember what questions he asked, or what I said to him, but having seen the Judge I do have a vague memory of seeing my mother in tears in the waiting room outside. I do not know precisely what she was crying about, but I do remember feeling a mixture of sadness at seeing her in distress and a degree of desperation too, thinking that if she could not cope with things, how on earth could we be expected to? This was one of several occasions on which I saw my mother break down in tears, such was the state of her emotional instability. In the end, custody was given to the local authority.

Life continued at the Paddocks until early in 1965, when a similar type of building came up for sale nearby. The owner of the Paddocks who had left to work elsewhere, decided to come back and start his own children's home there, hence the need to move to new premises.

This new building was called Lacton Hall and when it was first purchased, it necessitated some minor alterations and work done on it, to render it suitable for us children. Amongst other things that needed doing, were the varnishing of the wooden floors in the bedrooms. As a result, small groups of 2 or 3 of us children would go across there on Saturday mornings and earn some extra pocket money by varnishing these floors. Several months later, all the staff and the children of the Paddocks moved in.

Chapter 15
More Holidays

All of this term time life was punctuated by our continued holidays with the foster parents.

Among the good things we did with them, over the years, were trips to London to go to Kew Gardens, the Science Museum, the Ideal Home Exhibition (where we collected free samples and bought little gadgets like gyroscopes) and London Airport (now Heathrow). All these things brought us great enjoyment.

During these holidays we also continued to see our parents and from the relative security of staying with the foster parents it was possible, although perhaps not consciously so, to see both parents rather more objectively on these occasions. Although I was glad to see my parents, it was always with mixed feelings. My mother, who at this stage occupied a small but pleasant flatlet, was deteriorating both physically and mentally. Having had one nervous breakdown already, from which she had partially recovered, her emotional state was not a particularly healthy one. Nor indeed was her physical condition. This was partly as a result of having to take drugs such as Librium, and partly through her inability to eat food on occasions when under any great stress. She thereby grew terribly thin. These visits were not always particularly happy, as her condition naturally permeated our thoughts. Indeed, this ultimately led to her second nervous breakdown in 1968.

Nonetheless, on such visits, Dennis, who usually spent most evenings with my mother until he got married some years later, was always present and among the happier of these would be when he played his guitar and we would all sing, lark about and make tape recordings.

These visits to our parents were also fraught with other difficulties as further extracts from our files demonstrate.

"7 January 1963. Report by Mr M of conversations with foster father then with Colin and I en route to Victoria Station to go back to Caldecott for the beginning of term. Foster father said holiday comparatively successful, we had both behaved ourselves, and the limited visits had had some effect. On the other hand, each of the parents' attitude towards the reduced visits had made this difficult for us to accept. For example, our mother had made arrangements for us to go to her Works Christmas

party and she wrote a letter to Colin suggesting I asked the foster parents for their consent but adding that she would not ask the children's department as she knew what their answer would be! The foster parents did not agree to us going. Also, it seems our dad had said he might visit us during our last weekend and he might have done this but for the bad weather. In the car neither Colin or I could understand or accept the new restriction of visits to parents to one visit each holiday. Tony in particular was very unhappy and was near to crying. Colin was very much to the point in his questions about the restrictions and he asked, if the children's department really had our interests and happiness at heart, why they thought seeing our parents once only could help to make us feel more settled. Colin seemed to have received a bland answer and it was "plain, though unexpressed, that Colin did not appreciate this". He asked if we could spend holidays in a Children's Home in future, if meetings would be limited if we stayed with the Foster parents. Mr M appears to have put Colin's attitude down to our parents probably being jealous of the foster parents and working on us together with the fact that there is no one of his age near the foster home and he must feel the lack of such companionship."

Thus, by February of 1963 the local authority were saying that our stay with the foster parents was no longer tenable due to constant problems with our parents and therefore a new foster home would have to be found for us.

"6 February 1963. Reply by Miss S. to Miss Davies. Wondering if Miss Dave can suggest an alternative permanent holiday home for us, either in Kent or in another part of the country not easily accessible to the parents. Because of the parents' lack of cooperation and their undermining of any of our plans with which they do not agree, we must question the advisability of the boys continuing to stay with the foster parents for holidays. But for the poor weather during the Christmas holiday, there would almost certainly have been difficulties and we must consider the foster parents as well as the boys. Although not enthusiastic about the boys having another move, it would appear to be in their long-term interests. Not possible to reserve places for us in any of the Counties children's homes due to continual demand."

"11 March 1963. Reply Miss Davies to Miss S. Verbatim. I am sorry that you have had to write again about Colin and Tony Inwood's holiday arrangements. I had hoped that we would have had a visit from one of the parents this term so that I could feel more in the picture before answering you, but as I have not seen the foster parents nor the parents during the last two terms, it is difficult for me to assess the problem. I had a long talk with Colin this weekend and he is quite clear in his mind about the situation. He would rather remain at the foster parents, as it is quite the best holiday placement he has had. He does not want to be parted from Tony, but as neither his *father nor mother can afford to travel to Kent he feels it is perfectly reasonable to ask to see them at least once a week during the holidays. He realises that it is a problem for the foster parents, but implies that he thinks they should be asked to face this and put up with it. His only helpful suggestion is that they should not visit the parents on two consecutive days, but that as father is out of work they should spend Wednesday with him and Saturday with mother, and be with the foster parents throughout Sunday. I agree with you that a move is desirable and if we found them a home in this neighbourhood the boys would feel extremely cut off, as it is obvious the parents cannot face this long journey. Neither of the children want to return to a children's home in the holidays. As I cannot discuss matters with either the foster parents or the parents, I must leave it to you to make a decision."*

"14 March 1963. Reply Miss Davies to Miss S. Verbatim. I did not realise from either of your letters written on 6 February and 3 March, that the foster parents were not prepared to have the boys for the holidays. I regret their decision as it would appear that they have given considerable security to Colin and Tony during the last eighteen months. A foster home in this neighbourhood would not be a suitable arrangement, as it is obvious that the parents cannot afford to visit the boys at this distance. I must, therefore, ask you to make what arrangements you can in your area. I have one friend there and will

see if by any chance I can make any suggestion after contacting them."

"20 March 1963. Letters to Mum and Dad reinstating weekly visits for the Easter holiday, also adopting Colin's idea of Wednesdays to Dad."

"3 April 1963. Note of journey Victoria to Maidenhead. We told Mr M. once again that we would rather go to the foster parents than anywhere else, also that we were pleased to know that we would be seeing our parents more than once during the holidays. Colin told Mr M. that Tony was now at The Paddocks. Colin had made a wooden cross for foster father's birthday. He said that he had had a good term at school."

Happily for us, then, the local authority re-negotiated the situation with the foster parents and the visiting arrangements for parents were reinstated to weekly visits. However, yet another problem soon followed, regarding my father.

Chapter 16
Breakdown

My father's mental condition at this time, was also very poor. Having sold Coldridge Farm in 1960, he went to live with his brother, my Uncle George. He was invited to do this, partly, because Uncle George had lost his licence and needed someone to drive his milk van around making deliveries for him. This arrangement continued for about a year, until they had a disagreement over something, and my father left.

He then took a small suite of rooms at the top of a run-down old railway hotel in a nearby town and stayed there for about three years. It was here, that on 15 May 1964, the anniversary of his father's death, that he made a suicide attempt. However, by the grace of God, this proved unsuccessful. Apparently, he swallowed a large quantity of sleeping pills and in the middle of the night stormed around his room shouting and throwing around chairs and vomiting, until such time as the police were called.

This resulted is in his being compulsorily admitted to mental hospital. No doubt, because of having lived on his own and having brooded on the fate of his marriage and life as a whole, everything got too much for him. Whatever the reason, having stayed in hospital for the required period, he elected to stay on as a voluntary patient and remained there for some two months.

He then purchased a small caravan on a site nearby and lived there for about two years, whilst working in the gardens of another hospital. I believe he did this work voluntarily, because it provided him with something to do, which he enjoyed and gave him regular contact with people. This proved to be very therapeutic for him.

During this period, after the suicide attempt, my feelings of resentment towards my father largely subsided. I began to grow more sensitive towards him and also a little guilty for not writing to him more often during the term time.

Whilst he was living in the caravan, he needed to take various medications to keep him calm and I have a mental picture of this very sad old man, who felt he had nothing very much to live for, just idling through the rest of his life. Both Colin and I were very much aware of his condition at this stage and as result Colin suggested that we give him a special Christmas celebration that year to try and cheer him up a bit.

This took place on one of our visits to him during the Christmas holidays. We bought a cake and a bottle of ginger wine along with a small present from each of us and put these in a suitcase. We then made a special little banner about 3 feet long saying "Merry Christmas Dad" on it and packed that in the suitcase as well.

When we arrived at the caravan, having greeted him and talked for a few minutes, we told him that we had a surprise and that he was to wait in the bedroom part of the caravan whilst we prepared it. We then opened the suitcase and began to set everything up ready which, for some reason, took longer than we expected. After a while, he grew impatient and kept telling us to hurry up and wondered what we were doing, that took us so long. Finally, when all was ready with the cake complete with decoration, the ginger wine and the presents all laid out, the banner pinned up, plus one or two other decorations, we called him in.

As he came in, we wished him a "Happy Christmas" and as he looked around him his eyes filled with tears and he sat down, put his head in his hands and cried. He thanked us profusely, between sobs, for being so kind and after a few minutes, he wiped his eyes and apologised for breaking down in front of us. He then slowly began to enjoy a piece of cake and a glass of ginger wine.

He repeatedly told us throughout the rest of the day, how touched he was that we should care about him and for a long time afterwards would refer to the occasion, with a happy glint in his eye. For our part, we were really glad that it meant so much to him and having recovered from the initial shock of seeing him break down in tears, felt the whole thing was very worthwhile. In retrospect, I think this may well have given him the impetus he needed to get fully back on his feet.

Also, during this period, again at Colin's instigation, we decided to do whatever we could to make him happier and try and make our visits to him much more cheerful occasions than they had been in the past. As a result, we decided to try and keep up a steady flow of conversation with him instead of just allowing long periods of silence to develop, as they had done on previous occasions. One of the ways that we did this was to take along Colin's tape recorder from time to time and persuade him to sing into it some of the songs like "The Floral Dance" and "The Lord is my Shepherd", which he had sung at Coldridge Farm. We also recorded some of our conversations with him, on various subjects.

Around this time, he also let us learn to drive his car in a nearby field, which stood us both in good stead when the time came to start driving on the road. That way, we could then concentrate fully on the traffic and road signs etc., without having to learn to master the mechanics of driving at the same time.

As a result of this our relationship with him, on the whole, began to take on a more positive aspect, which was beneficial to us all. However, this was punctuated every now and then by the occasional row about something, which could sometimes seriously upset the atmosphere for the rest of the day.

On one occasion, I had a row with him about something on the last visit of the holiday and as he put us on the train back to our foster parents, I refused to say goodbye and just turned away and ignored him. I knew that he would be upset about this and felt terribly guilty afterwards, knowing that I would not see him for another three months. This whole incident began to escalate in my mind on the journey back and I was haunted by the thought that supposing he should die before I had a chance to see him and make it up again. As a result, I vowed never to row with him again.

Chapter 17
Move to the Vicarage

Despite the ups and downs and problems over parental visits, our holidays with the foster parents generally passed very happily and always at the end of each holiday we would feel really sad at leaving them and going back to Caldecott.

In some ways, things were going so well, that in 1964 they offered to keep me permanently living with them where I would attend a local school. I remember feeling very happy about this and really began to feel that being with the foster parents all the time would make a huge difference to the quality of my life.

The following extracts from our files refer to this issue.

"April 1964. File note by Mr H of visit to us at the foster parents. Not all readable. Colin is tall but slight in proportion, both of us enjoying our stay with the foster parents. Colin now wants to become a forestry officer

which he can do from his present school. He hopes to take maths English and science for GCE when he is sixteen. This is Tony's last term in the primary school at Caldecott. He is not sure whether he would like to go to a technical school with an agricultural bias. The foster parents think that Tony would like to leave Caldecott and live with them full-time and go to school locally. Colin said he would like to stay at Caldecott and the foster parents feel that we have both settled sufficiently for them to foster Tony full-time. The contact with our parents has worked out most satisfactorily this holiday."

"22 June 1964. Letter Mr H. to Miss Dave. It appears that from Easter onwards we travelled by coach from and to Victoria, not taken by Mr H. Reference to a recent telephone conversation in which he conveyed to Miss Dave an offer by the foster parents, which appears to be for Tony to leave Caldecott and to live permanently with them. Mr H. wanting to know Miss Dave's view of Tony's best interests and saying that for his part he has the security of both of us in mind and that if Tony is well settled and happy at Caldecott, he would be reluctant to make any change that would disturb Tony. Father still having treatment in Park Prewitt mental hospital, where he was admitted last month."

"2 July 1964. Letter Miss Dave replying to foster father. Been considering us a lot this term, vis: the suggestion that Tony leave Caldecott to live with the foster parents; have

been thinking that Tony would do well to follow Colin into secondary school, where he has made a very good start and is very happy; then a report of Mum visiting (appears to be 21 June) and giving a pitiful picture of Dad's mental breakdown, which apparently we did know of. Also, that Mum was against Tony leaving Caldecott, especially when her husband is in hospital and she is trying to get through her divorce, she feels her husband might interfere with the boys and cause trouble. Miss Dave understands that Dad is unable to return to the Railway Hotel. The proposal for the holiday in September, it would be bad for Tony to miss the first two weeks in a new school, and for Colin to lose ground. She will discuss all these matters with children's department for their advice. She too is sorry to have so little contact with the foster parents and that they have been unable to visit.

26 August 1964. Notes of Mr H visit to us at foster parents. Saw us in our bedroom, where we have two tier bunkbeds. We had enjoyed our holiday, clearly regard the foster home as our home, as this room was very much our headquarters, and from seeing us together and from what the foster parents said, we get on well with each other. On odd occasions, when Colin was doing a few hours work at the bus station, the foster parents would take Tony out on his own which they felt he appreciated."

"30 August 1964. Letter foster parents to Miss Dave (replying to a letter not on the file). Then verbatim "Tony

has enjoyed his holiday, he fits in with our own boys very well, organising their games very well! Unfortunately, the gap between Colin and Tony seems wider and I am afraid that Colin has been rather bored. However, he is getting on well at school and seems to be growing up fast, so I suppose he is bound to find our household rather juvenile!".

"17 June 1965. Letter Mr H. to Miss Dave. He is leaving children's department at beginning of July. Divorce case: father was granted the divorce (in March); no order as to custody, as in the care of children's department and the arrangements considered to be satisfactory. The foster parents have now moved to a nearby village as the foster father has now been made Vicar of the Church there."

Thus, it was finally decided for a variety of reasons that I would be better off remaining at Caldecott and going out to school from there. Naturally, at first, I was very disappointed at this decision, but grew to accept it and ultimately it did not detract from my enjoyment of future holidays with the foster parents.

Thus in 1965, John was appointed as Vicar of his own church in a very attractive village a few miles from where they lived. After many years as a curate, both he and Margaret were delighted about this and they moved into the Vicarage, which was a splendid old house with a lot of rooms. It had a tennis court and a lawn at the back in fairly extensive grounds. It also backed onto the river at one point and was a superb country house. Naturally, we too came here during the holidays, and were thrilled to each be given our own room, for which we could each choose the colour scheme. This move more or less coincided with my transfer from the Paddocks to Lacton Hall.

Chapter 18
Lacton Hall

It was a little unsettling to think we had to move from The Paddocks to new premises. However, that soon evaporated because of the sorties we had made to our new home to help with the preparation of the house in the previous term. It also meant that we had thoroughly familiarised ourselves with the house and grounds before we actually took up residence.

So, we soon found that, as with the Paddocks, life at Lacton Hall was good. Upon our arrival we were met by a 3-legged Siamese cat, called "Tripod"! This was an intriguing animal who had belonged to the previous owner and for some reason had stayed on at the house. Tripod was a nice addition to having the lovely Tosca, James and Tessa's dog, who had been at the Paddocks too. Later another new arrival was that of Bella, a big brown mastiff with an overshot bottom jaw. She was very cuddly and friendly, especially as a young puppy, and was a delight to have around. All this was then crowned wonderfully when Tosca mated with another dog in the area by mistake and produced a large litter of puppies of mixed colours. These were a delight to everyone and were housed in the garage next to James and Tessa's VW Camper Van, which was known as "Luther"!

One thing that we missed at Lacton Hall was the little "Duck Pond" swimming pool which had proved so successful at the Paddocks. So, James decided to build another one in the garden and there were gangs of us who would help to dig up the earth and then wheel it round to the meadow at the back and then dump it in any little hollows to make the area more level. By the time the pool was finished, it proved to be even better than the old duck pond and was a great source of fun in the summer months. The next step was to make a cricket pitch in the meadow, which now had far less bumps in it, thanks to all the swimming pool earth that been dumped there. The pitch was a rather rough and ready affair, but it did the job and was used a lot for practising our cricket skills.

A few of us then thought about replicating the idea of a tree house, like we had before, but then instead, had the idea of digging out an underground camp on the edge of the field. This camp was in fact only half underground as we used the earth that we dug out to build up a little wall all around the top and then put on a roof of branches, corrugated iron and earth. Still, it was fun to build and fun to use.

We were allowed to watch more TV at Lacton Hall than over at Hatch, the main House, and we felt a little superior as a result! This was still in the days of black and white TV, of course. I remember watching programmes such as Blue Peter, The Man from Uncle, various cartoons and Top of the Pops. On Saturday evenings we always watched Bonanza (a cowboy series) and each had a packet of crisps to munch on, whilst doing so.

Other enjoyable summer activities were having occasional barbeques in the courtyard, with Tessa cooking sausages by the score. Then we had a "Pick Your Own" Farm over the road and sometimes we would go and pick strawberries to earn some extra money and sometimes we would go over in the evenings when it was closed and just help ourselves to the strawberries and then take them back and gorge ourselves silly on them!

After we had been at Lacton Hall for some time, James did a social work course at Oxford for a while, which involved working in another children's home. This meant that he would go up on a Sunday evening and stay there all week and return on a Friday evening. We all missed him a great deal during the week, but as Friday approached there would be mounting excitement about his return. As soon as he was spotted, the word was out and children would race to greet him and he was jumped on by a jubilant crowd of them. His wife and family had to wait their turn before welcoming back husband and father! In retrospect it is clear to me, and other children who were there, that the sharing of their own family life with the wider Lacton Hall (and Paddocks) family must at times have caused some degree of stress for them. However, the personal cost to them was never communicated to us, and they simply absorbed it.

I think the reason that James was so popular with us children was partly that he was very easy going and partly because he was a kind of father figure and treated us with a great deal of emotional warmth and kindness. He was also almost endlessly patient when tantrums were thrown by any of us and he managed to soak up a good deal in the way of aggression. He was almost always good humoured and simply great fun. I still recall many little anecdotes he would tell us about life and people and things that he had done in the past, which was very entertaining.

I remember being terribly proud once when he came along to my open day at school one year, as neither my parents, nor foster parents were in a position to do so. When he saw the wrought iron gate that I had made in my metalwork class, he bought it from me for a very generous sum. He subsequently had that gate in his cottage garden for very many years.

On Sunday mornings, like at the Paddocks, we went to Chapel at Hatch. This meant piling into "Luther", (James and Tessa's VW camper van) for the 10-minute trip. At that time, I didn't really like the idea of going to Chapel (although I am a Christian now), so I would protest in the strongest possible terms! However, gentle authority always won out. In retrospect I did enjoy certain parts of it though. I recall listening to the senior girls' choir beautifully singing the Lord's Prayer and various Psalms under the guidance of Betty Rayment, the music teacher. So, despite my protestations, it still managed to permeate my being to a certain extent.

Then on Sunday evenings, once again, we had "Reading". This was alternated with group singing, with James on guitar and he and Tessa leading us all in some folk songs before going off to bed. Another cosy way to round off the weekend.

During this period of my life, I began to make contact with a man called Simon Rodway, who, later on, was to play a very important part in my life and indeed still does. Simon at this time, was a Child Care Officer, and worked for a London Borough. A few years previously, however, he had worked at Caldecott as a housemaster for 14 to 18-year-old boys.

Although I occasionally saw him when I first arrived at Caldecott, I had very little to do with him at that time being so young, (I was in the Junior Study). However, whilst I was at Lacton Hall, he made regular visits to see a friend of mine who was then directly under his charge, as Simon was his CCO. Simon, however, whilst officially visiting to look after this boy's needs, would spread himself around a bit as he had a great love of children generally and he always spent some time with lots of us and was very popular.

Very often when he came down, he would take my friend out for a meal and would sometimes include me or some other child in the outing. These meals were usually held in hamburger bars or similar restaurants and provided a real highlight to our lives from time to time. This was not just because of the food, but the sense of occasion and the jollity of Simon's company, which always managed to make us feel cheerful. Thus, his visits once or twice a term were always looked forward to by number of children, not directly involved with him, but who felt a great degree of affinity with him and much enjoyed his company.

My own connection with Simon at this stage was slightly more vivid too, in that my brother, who had left Caldecott, was working in London and often called in after work to visit Simon in his flat in Shepherds Bush. This provided me with more of a basis for contact with Simon as well. Also, during the school holidays, I spent one or two evenings with Colin and Simon in London, in order to have a meal or see a film. Simon always paid for these outings and we would often then stay the night and return to the foster parents, the following morning, where Colin was now living full-time. These evenings at Simon's flat were always great fun and extremely enjoyable. Eventually, Colin moved into the flat with Simon, which was also shared with another old Caldecott boy.

So, the happy family atmosphere continued at Lacton Hall, as it had done so well, at the Paddocks. However, at this stage, my life had become increasingly marred by the various problems that had been rumbling on in the background for years.

Chapter 19
Hanging On

At this stage of my life, the problems with the foster parents had re-emerged and loomed ever larger, so it wasn't long before we came to an inevitable crisis point. The following extracts from the files best illustrate the sequence of events that led up to this.

"8ᵗʰ March 1966. File note of a Child Care Officer visit to foster parents. Met only foster father. He said that Tony was just the same as he always had been, and nobody had ever really managed to get anywhere near him, and he obviously found it difficult to confide in people."

"4ᵗʰ January 1967. File note by CCO of visit to foster parents. She first saw Tony on his own. He is very hard work to talk to and confines his conversation strictly to answering what he is asked and will not give away anything. Foster mother told her that they are worried about Tony, and always have been, saying that he is very withdrawn. It has become worse in the last year or 18

months. He spends most of his time in his own room and joins in very little with the family. She appreciates that her own children are rather young for Tony.

In previous years Tony had brought Christmas presents for her children but not this year. She felt this to be significant and had always felt that Tony and Colin had stayed with them rather than living with them. Foster mother felt that the situation with Tony would not have developed had she been allowed to have him with her all the time rather than him going away to school. Tony has no friends in the area and apart from going to table tennis with Colin does not join in anything and does very little with his leisure time. It transpired that Tony had not brought the children Christmas presents because he had been fined several times at Caldecott for smoking."

"2nd March 1967. CCO visit to foster mother following visit to Caldecott. Little achieved. She still feeling that Tony would be better off elsewhere for his holidays unless he could leave Caldecott and live with them permanently. CCO concerned that a change of school for a fourteen-year-old not good but foster mother did not appear to attach much importance to this."

Then followed a re-awakening of the convoluted negotiations about my potential chances of remaining with the foster parents. However, this was juxtaposed with a confusing mixture of oscillating ideas about mine and indeed Colin's future with them.

"1 April 1967. Letter foster mother to Children's Dept. After the present holiday I shall not be able to care for the Inwood boys. Reasons: for some months life with them had been very difficult; the house divided into two camps; the happy atmosphere ruined; chief problem is that Tony and Colin do not wish to join in family life; also difficulties of visits to Mother. Would be better if other arrangements made for Tony's holidays. Last week Mother sent them back here at 12.30pm with no telephone message. Last night they did not return at all as they were "too sick to travel" after drinking too much. I must put the stability of my family first. I hope you will be able to find a place for Tony where he will be happier. Colin will be 18 in May and, presumably, independent. He continues to work in London and I imagine will live there."

"6 April 1967. CCO file note. Verbatim. Took Tony with me on a visit to a child in Woking in order to have a long opportunity of getting him to talk to me. Found him very thoughtful and quite perceptive for his age. He is also extremely anxious about the possible breakdown of his fostering in the household and asked me two or three times during the day whether he was going to have to leave. Was able to talk to him about the antagonism between his mother and foster mother and to explain it

from both points of view and he appeared to understand this quite readily."

"9th April 1967. Letter from foster mother to CCO. Verbatim. Sorry to bother you again but I learned yesterday that Mrs Inwood is intending to move to a town nearby. She has written for a job and flat, I believe. I am sure that you will realise that this places a very different complexion on things. We do not feel able to have Tony living here if mother is nearby. I am sorry to add to the difficulties, but after seven years of deceit instigated by her and the present difficulties, I am afraid that that would be more than we could cope with. I do not know if Tony knows that she is thinking of this move, he has not said anything about it to us. I'm not sure we have got the position quite clear but I do feel that if she moves nearby, Tony should definitely go elsewhere, which alters my original conditions about Caldecott etc. Do hope you will manage to sort some of the problems out soon."

"25 April 1967. Letter foster father to CCO. Extract verbatim. We had very little success with Tony during the last days of the holiday and feel that we must insist on his being found alternative foster parents for his future holidays. As you know, we think that he needs the company of boys of his own age, and a place where the influence of his mother can be less than it is here."

The following shows very well the mental state of my mother and father at this juncture.

"27 April 1967. CCO Miss G notes of meetings with Mum and then Dad.

Mum. Verbatim extracts.

I was about an hour late in arriving for this interview and found the scene set for an intimate, almost social, occasion. There was a daintily laid tray of tea and biscuits. Mrs Inwood insisted that I take my coat off and she was obviously prepared to enjoy the occasion. This impression was confirmed at the end of the two-hour interview when she expressed some disillusionment.

A thin grey-haired person, with a perpetually mournful expression and manner of speaking, Mrs. Inwood's emotional disturbance became obvious during the first few minutes of conversation. Not once during the two-hour conversation did she appear able to see anything other than from her own point of view and the effect which it had upon her. The object of my visit .... to explain why the visits from Tony needed to be curtailed and to enlist her cooperation in the event of Tony needing to leave the foster parents, in any other plan which might be made for him................ She tended continually to digress onto her feelings with regard to the way in which Dennis, her elder son, treated her by getting married to a girl whom she does not approve of. Frequent references to her cruel treatment from her husband and the way in which she has suffered and sacrificed in order to do her best for the boys. The terrible hardship Tony's placement at Caldecott has caused her and how it is impossible for her to visit him during term time because it does such awful things to her nerves.

She views the boys' visits with morbid sentimentality – for instance, the fact that after Colin has been to see her, she leaves the two cups that they have used on the draining board for several days together with the ash tray that he used."

Mother

She sat there, opposite me,
in the scruffy little café
near the school bus stop.

Shall we put something on the Juke Box?
She asked.
She loved pop music.
How about "What a Wonderful World"
and "Whiter Shade of Pale"?

I put them on.
Can't remember what we talked about.
I do recall feeling sad for her though,
but not in a condescending way.

She always wanted me to call her mum,
but I felt uncomfortable with that.
It's so hard and strange,
to see your own mother sinking
before your very eyes.

At this stage in his life, my father had sold his caravan and bought a bungalow and a new car and was very much on the up. He had lodgers and used to take them on days out occasionally, as they had no car themselves. The bungalow had a good-sized garden, which he much enjoyed working in and he grew flowers and vegetables in it. In fact, he once dug up a potato, that was Three-in-one, and the local paper had a photo of him holding the potato with a little caption underneath it. He was thrilled.

About this time, he gave us a studio photo of himself one Christmas, which he said would be a memento of him when he died.

"Later I went to see Mr. Inwood. He was very angry. I let him go on for about 10 minutes on the preposterousness of the idea of restricting a child's visits to the father he loved so dearly - he had never heard such a scandalous idea and he was not going to stand for it. I apologised for not having come to see him about it before he learned about it from Tony and tried to explain why it was necessary.

Mr. Inwood's emotional disturbance, like that of his wife's, becomes apparent very early in conversation - like her his thoughts are almost entirely self-centred and everything is related to the (effect?) which it has on his nerves. This is his reason for not being able to visit Tony during term time. As he talked he looked constantly at one chair which must be where Tony sits. Mr. Inwood was however more susceptible to reason than his wife and after (??) hours was able to at least partially see the problem from Tony's point of (view?) and to promise cooperation.

Although my contribution to the interview with him was much the same as it had been with Mrs. Inwood, he saw, and was impressed by, what he said he felt to be sincere concern for Tony. Mrs. Inwood has only seen (xxxxxxxxxx) a direct attempt at personal injury to herself.

Mr. Inwood lives in a bungalow of which one room is let to a young couple. It is very much "man-kept" and I could detect no signs of a woman taking any part in his life. He said that Tony could come to live with him although providing a young boy with meals was going to be a terrible strain on his "nerves". He himself hasn't eaten a proper meal for years. He doesn't look as though (suffering?) from malnutrition.

In telling me how cruel his wife has been in trying to influence the boys against him, he made a most significant remark: "I told the boys when they were young that I hoped they would always find that they were (able?) to love their mother". Mr. Inwood wanted to know exactly what time I would be starting out on my next visit to Caldecott so that "I can think of you on your (journey?) to visit my dear boy".

Chapter 20
Denouement

As I had recently become more involved with Simon Rodway, because of his visits to Lacton Hall, he had begun to take an interest in my affairs over the foster parents and was keen to help out in any way he could.

"1 May 1967. CCO letter to Mr Rodway about the negotiations between the Children's Department and the foster parents. A brief update on the situation about Tony, that the outcome is impossible to say at this stage, she will let him know when any plan has been formulated. Then "your continued cooperation in keeping yourself as uninvolved as possible would be most appreciated, the situation being so complicated".

8 May 1967. CCO letter to Mr Rodway replying to a letter 3rd May not on the file. "The foster parents' rejection of Tony is now final and if you call at Caldecott next week, I think you will find Tony rather stunned, even though he had been half expecting this"."

"10 May 1967. Letter from Simon to CCO on headed paper. "I was at Caldecott yesterday and agree that Tony seemed rather stunned by the foster parents' rejection. I felt very sorry for him, as the outlook isn't too hopeful"."

"10 May 1967. Identical CCO letters to mum and dad. Verbatim. I regret to say that the foster parents have finally decided not to have Tony for his holidays again. Mr. E and I saw Tony last week as planned and feel he must be given time to adjust to the situation before making any attempt to form an alternative plan for him. He will be helped by Mr. King to do his own thinking about this and we will be keeping in close touch with Caldecott. I will let you know as soon as a decision has been reached."

"10 May 1967. The foster parents had been asked if they would write to Tony making the situation clear to him and this they have done."

Thus, my years with the foster parents - years that had brought much in the way of joy and angst, finally came to an end and I began to nose-dive, became more isolated and subject to bouts of depression. I also developed an underlying feeling of anger and resentment, and no doubt a degree of self-pity along with it. I felt cheated by life and wanted to strike back at my misfortune. So, to my shame, I deliberately became very anti-social and went on shoplifting sprees with a few other friends, embarked on various acts of delinquency and even broke into houses on a couple of occasions.

Chapter 21
Turmoil

Then began the tortuous process of finding holiday placements for me. The following extracts show how Caldecott and the Children's Department bent over backwards to try and sort it all out for me. However, due to my somewhat extreme mental and emotional state at the time I was unable to appreciate it.

"26 May 1967. Mr King letter to Miss G. Replying about the arrangements for her visit. Then "he (Tony) has not had a very good spell, though I hope he is steadier again now. He was involved in selling stolen raffle tickets and buying cigarettes with the proceeds. He also did some petty shop lifting at Woolworths and he has been smoking heavily. He has made a big effort this last week not to smoke and I think the other things are not in themselves a cause for concern. He is however very anxious about next term and going to our Colt House. He still sticks to the words of Mr. E that he has a choice of whether he stays at the Caldecott or not. What he

doesn't know is what the alternative is going to be and at the present moment he won't completely accept the alternative as I have put it to him. I'm sure and not without reason, he thinks I am biased. Perhaps you or Mr. E can put him in the picture in the near future."

"5 June 1967. CCO filenote of telephone call from Mr King. Verbatim. Tony has recently done some shoplifting from Woolworths and while camping over half-term, spoiled a visitors' book, attempted to pull a poor box off the wall and spoiled some candles in a church. This morning was picked up at Ashford station at 1am. with platform ticket in pocket in the company of younger boy 12 years of age, who is already referred for psychiatric help because of delinquent tendencies. This association is fairly recent. (I think he and I fed on each other's destructive emotions). *Tony has said he would like to go pony trekking. Staff at Caldecott are waiting to move Tony to the Colt House within the next day or two and Mr. King asked for a letter confirming that we have no immediate plans for him.*

5 June 1967. Letter Children's Department to Miss Davies. Confirming a telephone conversation Miss G with Mr King. No plans for Tony yet. Miss G is making contact with Miss R, Area Children's Officer Ashford and then hopes to visit Tony shortly."

"*7 June 1967. CCO filenote. Verbatim. Visited foster parents to collect the rest of Tony's belongings. Saw foster father first and he asked me whether we had been able to assess Tony's reaction when we last visited him. Told him that Tony had seen us and the letter simultaneously and that Tony had been quite shattered and that since then I could only say that he had been kicking against the world pretty badly. Foster father said that he had always been doing that and I assured him that it had been nothing like his recent behaviour.* (I don't quite know what he meant by that comment. I was definitely withdrawn then, but certainly not delinquent.) *I didn't go into any details as to what Tony had been doing. When foster mother joined us she made no enquiries and never once looked me? straight in the eye. No attempt had been made to put Tony's things together neatly - they had been literally thrown into a cardboard box. Colin was there as well and there was no message for Tony from any one of the them or any enquiries as to his wellbeing.*

There is a CCO file note, too faint to read properly, of a report from Mr King which appears to be saying that Tony's delinquent behaviour has included a "couldn't care less attitude about what happened to him". Then suddenly one day, when somebody told him to stop being so sorry for himself, this produced tears followed by Tony being able suddenly to talk about his feelings of rejection by the foster parents."

"13 June 1967. CCO letter to Area Children's Officer Miss R following up on a discussion about whether they might be able to find foster parents for the school holidays. It includes the following description of Tony. "Tony has been rejected by his foster parents after 7 years for complicated reasons, in which Tony himself played little part. It has been strongly felt for some time that Tony was pulled many ways, with a parent in each of two different places, foster parents in another and Caldecott in Kent, and not one of them very much liking the other. Tony has said that he would like another foster home."

Not surprisingly, my emotions and thoughts about the future, in as much as I was able to think realistically about that, ricocheted and at times bordered on desperation.

"13 June 1967. A varied list of possibilities in the making for Tony's summer holidays, drawn up by the CCO, including possibly staying with Mr. and Mrs. King, camping in Brittany, locally with a school friend, with a Mr. John Allen, and a variety of youth hostels and similar."

"13 June 1967. Letter Miss G to Mr and Mrs King. Confirming visit findings. How pleased she is with Tony. Pleased he wants to stay and that he is more open-minded about a move soon to the Colt House. Advertising for a foster home in Kent. Feels Tony will be better off centring his life in one place in future. Some practicalities about summer holiday stays away being arranged for Tony."

"3 July 1967. Letter Dennis (My eldest brother) *to CCO offering to take Tony for one week during the summer holidays touring in the west country."*

"11 July 1967. CCO file note telephone conversation with Mr King. Verbatim. He seems angry with the Department. Said Tony also angry with us as feels they are trying to get rid of him. Mr. King's suggestion – Tony be allowed to spend part of each holiday with mother as she suggests. Asked him how long he thinks this would last and what chance there would be to make any permanent holiday (xxxxxxx placement?) for Tony. Said would go somewhere else for other bit of holiday. No suggestion where. Feels Tony being pushed around rather. If mother has him out of (xxxxxx care?) says could offer free place at Caldecott. Wants to keep pony trekking holiday, Caldecott to pay, if Tony discharged. Taken it for granted Tony was going to mother for a fortnight and with Dennis for a week. Says visit to school friend may have to be cancelled."

"14 July 1967. Two-page file note CCO visit to Tony and Mr King. First page too feint to read. Second page verbatim extracts. Mrs Inwood will be having her annual holiday during the fortnight that Tony is with her. During this conversation I asked Tony if he still wanted to talk about the reasons why he had to leave the foster parents, to this he replied "What is the use? It's all over now, isn't it?" I then saw Mr. King with Tony and found that he also, as

I had anticipated, was quite angry with the Children's Department, having interpreted my calling of mother's bluff on previous occasions with regard to her threat of removing Tony from care, as a loss of interest by us in Tony, although this had been explained to him on the first occasion."

"19 July 1967. CCO letter to my father, updating him about holiday arrangements. Mrs. Inwood had said she wanted to discharge Tony from care, however since then Tony does not seem to want to be discharged but she is not sure how his mother will feel about this.

Setting out the present plans for Tony's holiday, which are pony trekking in Gloucester, a stay with Mrs. King's father, five days with Dennis and his wife in the west country, the last two weeks or so with his mother. She feels sure that Tony will be down to see his father during that period.

21 July 1967. CCO file note. Met Tony at the main office and took him to Childrens' home in Gloucestershire for pony trekking holiday. Personal transport in this instance was deliberate as I felt that he was still needing to talk. I had not intended to mention any of our vague suspicions of an element of matrimonial disharmony in the foster family but when I asked Tony if he felt that foster father might have been prepared for him to remain there, Tony replied without hesitation, "Yes. If he did not give in to foster mother every time there would not be any marriage there. It would have bust up years ago". Tony having made these observations, I was able to point out how much more difficult it was to incorporate foster children into the family under these circumstances and how the presence of others could in fact aggravate the existing tension."

This points up the fact that the foster parents were having problems in their marriage, which may have been going on to a greater or lesser degree for some time. Clearly this had an effect on their relationship with us and was causing Margaret to behave in a somewhat volatile way in her views of us and her decisions about us.

Colin, at this stage, was keen on his schoolwork and wanting to make a real go of things and build a career for himself. As far as I was concerned, I was beginning to recover emotionally from recent events, but was still to some extent, in a state of limbo.

I have to say in retrospect, however, that the foster parents did give us a great deal whilst we were with them over a good many years, despite the problems and I still have some very warm and happy memories of my years with them.

"Sympathising with him that he had all these things to cope with before he was grown up and pointing out that

some children did and some didn't, Tony produced a very interesting comment, "I'll have a head start on a lot of other kids, won't I?" Agreed with him wholeheartedly and said that I had been both surprised and very pleased at the mature way in which he had coped with all the difficulties of the past few months. Told him I had heard about his little outburst of bad behaviour but understood and had not said anything about it at the time and that I was glad that he had got over it quickly, had stopped being sorry for himself and could see that he was obviously thinking very positively now. These comments caused Tony to be somewhat overcome with embarrassment but seemed to please him."

This pony trekking holiday was supposed to be for a fortnight, but in the event, turned out to be for one week only. The first week was spent in the children's home in Gloucestershire and the deputy head was a man called John Allen. The pony trekking took place in Wales and passed off reasonably well. John Allen seemed kind to me and gave me a lot of his attention, although I did feel a little uncomfortable with him in some ways.

Nonetheless, he told me that he ran a hotel in Wrexham and that if I wanted, when I left school, that I could go and work in his hotel and train for hotel management. This idea appealed to me quite a lot and I began to feel for a short period that things might work out well for me here. It was arranged for me to have a short stay at his hotel on a subsequent occasion to see what I thought. However, when I was there, I began to see a very different side to him.

Anyway, it turned out that this man subsequently set up a group of children's homes called the Bryn Alyn Community, was found guilty of numerous charges of sexual abuse on boys over many years and is currently serving a life sentence. Clearly, I had a very narrow escape.

Chapter 22
The Colt House

The Colt House was a separate unit in the grounds at Hatch, adjacent to the main house and provided living accommodation for the senior boys between 14 to 18 years old. I wasn't especially looking forward to going there, as the man who ran it at that time was rather disciplinarian and, to put it politely, lacked empathy. This was in complete contrast to the Paddocks and Lacton Hall under the aegis of James and Tessa King.

Fortunately for me, my first term in the Colt House happened to be the last term that this man was in charge. I think that knowledge helped me to adapt to the new system and because he knew his tenure there was not going to last, he mellowed a little according to those boys who had been with him for several terms.

So, life was a bit different for me, to say the least. However, the one positive thing that I did benefit from whilst he was there, as did many of us boys, was the great tuition and encouragement he gave with sports, notably for me, playing table tennis. I really loved that game and it was a great source of stimulation. He also got the Community to upgrade their sports equipment.

When he left, another more lenient man took over and the regime, if I may call it that, was very much more relaxed. So, thankfully we were given more in the way of freedom in order to encourage us to take a little more responsibility for our own lives and this was manifested in various ways, one of which was that we were given a clothing allowance. This could be spent on more or less whatever we chose. This was just what we craved especially as it was the height of the "Flower Power" era and the chance to try and look and dress like the Beatles, Pink Floyd or other pop groups that I thought seemed really fabulous.

So, on a Saturday afternoon we would go to Ashford, unsupervised and go to a film at the Odeon (James Bond always seemed to feature prominently!) and then blow our allowance on the most outrageous outfits we could lay our hands on. I recall buying once a bright yellow corduroy suit and then very flowery zip up shirts to go with it.

Wrangler jackets were all the rage at that time too and as the months went by, I used to supplement my new clothing style by making my own, (very crude) clothes.

I once found an old coat in a dressing up box and added some very frilly cuffs to it and dyed it mauve, and then dyed some old jeans orange to go with it!

This new freedom for clothes was made even better by the fact that we were also allowed to grow our hair a bit longer, which was such a relief after years of "short back and sides". Indeed, I considered any form of haircut at that time to be an abomination, so the new style and look was just great. Perhaps the pinnacle of this new-found freedom, though, was the chance to wear our newly bought psychedelic gear into supper on a Saturday night rather than the dreadful blue and grey uniform that we were given - freedom indeed!!

As for other recreational activities at that time, I suppose it was inevitable given the explosion of pop music, that quite a few of us had guitars and tried to master them by playing 3 chords (probably not terribly well!) and trying desperately to enter the spirit of the times. Ultimately it was folk music that took precedence over everything else, and this was really due to John, an old boy, who worked locally, and spent a lot of his leisure hours at Hatch. He actually did master his guitar very well and we would have great sing-songs of Pete Seeger, Tom Paxton et al in the little lounge room at the front of the Colt House and one boy would sing really enthusiastically into his hockey stick, which was a most imaginative microphone!

John, who also used to help out in the boiler room in the evenings and weekends, no doubt enjoyed the camaraderie of us Colt House lads. He would sometimes supply us, rather reluctantly, with a few of his Players No.6 cigarettes and was great to have around.

His main job was working for a local engineering firm in Ashford and this came in very useful in my last term at Hatch, because he had the idea to make a Go-Kart by using an old moped engine attached to a very grand soap box style trolley. We lads thought this was brilliant and we mucked in with him to help build it. It was so good when he would come back triumphantly from work some evenings and produce from his bag, with a great flourish, a gear stick that he had made or some pedal for the brakes and accelerator. He was a real inspiration to us.

Finally, when the Go-Kart was completed, we all took turns to drive it round the grounds of Hatch with the engine roaring, the whole thing vibrating with what seemed like enormous power and a crowd of spectators to share in the fun!

Another freedom that was bestowed on us too, was that Chris, a good friend of mine who had also been at the Paddocks and Lacton Hall, was allowed to buy a second hand Lambretta Scooter from a mate of his at Ashford Grammar. He took great delight in haring around the place on this "Mod Machine", but wasn't the slightest bit concerned about safety, or so it seemed. One day he went roaring off down the switchback at great speed and when he got to the bottom was going too fast to take the bend, so he slammed on the brakes in an effort to do a broadside, skidded spectacularly on the loose gravel and came flying off onto the grass and a bunch of stinging nettles! Mercifully he was largely unhurt apart from a few bruises, but it did rather put him off the idea of having a scooter and he subsequently sold it to me!

My skills at riding were not much better than his, however, but were decidedly slower. One day when out on the road I was following a bus into Ashford. It so happened that there, looking out of the back window at the top of the bus, were a few of the Colt House Chaps, who started waving and jeering at me on my new machine. My attention was, therefore, somewhat diverted at that point and as I waved back enthusiastically, I didn't notice that the bus was coming to a stop. Thus, I very nearly went smack into the back of it. Fortunately for me, I was then given some very sound advice by a passing policeman who strongly advised that I get a lot of off-road practice on the machine before unleashing myself on the unwitting public again!

One form of encouragement and loose discipline that was in place for 14-year-olds and upwards, was a system of privileges. This was known as "Privileged Uniform" (PU for short). So, if a child had behaved responsibly during the week and had not been caught indulging in smoking or other naughty things, then they had their name announced at Saturday supper as being a PU for the week ahead. This carried with it such privileges as going to bed half an hour later than normal, being able to make coffee after supper and other small things like that.

The bedtimes were really very early for us in those days, I am not sure why, so the extra half hour really was most welcome. My record of achieving my PU, however, was not overly successful! For those whose record was consistent, though, there was the supreme honour of becoming a "Permanently Privileged Uniform (PPU) and that meant, in effect, being a prefect and having some minor authority over the other boys, as well as all the privileges. Needless to say, I never managed to achieve that lofty status!

Another aspect of the routine here was "Runs and Showers". This meant rising at 7am and going for a 10-minute run in just shorts and gym shoes (trainers) and took place all year round, unless there was snow and ice on the ground. After that we had a supervised 10 second cold shower. This routine all came about because Miss Leila, who was very friendly with Kurt Hahn, the founder of Gordonstoun, was persuaded by him to institute this early morning exercise for us in the belief that it was character building. After that, we got dressed, did a brief morning job of housework before breakfast and school. Interestingly, Caldecott also had a bursary fund provided by a member of staff, which meant that occasionally a boy could be sent to Gordonstoun, if Miss Leila thought they would benefit from it.

So, life in the Colt House continued with its ups and downs and there was the inevitable background of problems for me, in other areas of life, which came to bear very painfully during the remainder of my time at Caldecott.

Chapter 23
Dad

A very fortunate thing happened in April 1968, which was a brief time of reconciliation between my mother and father. This was a great blessing.

> "19 April 1968. CCO file note. Mr. and Mrs. Inwood are now on friendly terms. I was told that at Christmas, Mr. and Mrs. Inwood, Dennis, Colin and Tony were together for half an hour at Mr Inwood's home. They had had a drink, before which Mrs. Inwood had said "there were faults on both sides"."

Among the other happier memories of this period, was my father's 60th birthday a few months earlier. No doubt, having fond memories of the Christmas celebration that Colin and I gave him a year or two prior to that, he was most keen that we should join with him to celebrate, what to him was going to be a monumental occasion. He wrote to Miss Dave, asking permission for me to be with him for it and to spend a night or two there as it took place during term time. He was delighted to have survived to this great age, as he saw it, especially in view of what he described as the many sad and unhappy years that had led up to it.

"25 September 1967. Letter Dad (address St Martins) to Miss Dave. I have just heard from Tony asking me to write to ask your permission for him to come home next weekend, for my very special 60th birthday on Saturday 30th September. I feel it is so very special as with all the sad years and deep depression it is only by the Grace of God I am still breathing. Will you please grant him permission to come. I hope you and Miss Rendel are keeping well. Yours sincerely, Cyril Inwood. PS I was very proud that Colin and Tony were chosen to talk about the Caldecott Community on Southern TV."

This reference to Southern TV (which no longer exists) was to a series of late evening social documentary type programmes, called "Epilogue". The theme for one of the weeks was a five-episode programme about the Caldecott Community, hosted by Simon Rodway. In it he interviewed various members of staff and some old boys. My brother, Colin, was one such interviewee and spoke of the difficulties he experienced in adapting to life in the outside world when he left Caldecott. My role in it was to read a short piece from the "Caldecott Charter", which was played at the opening of each episode. The piece in question was:

"Above all, remembering that the community exists in common with all mankind, solely that it may go forward on an eternal quest, forever seeking to discover God's purpose for his world and for each individual soul in his world".

Naturally, I was very keen to see it and that particular episode was being screened on the first night of term. However, as I started school a day later than the other boys, I asked the man in charge of the Colt House if I could stay up and watch it. Sadly, he turned my request down flat. When I asked him why, he simply said, "Because it's way past your bedtime, that's why". Argument was completely useless, and I never did see the programme. Fortunately, my mother did record an audio version on her reel-to-reel tape recorder, so I did at least get to hear it.

It is my belief that during those years my father must have experienced many feelings of guilt and isolation, and he probably had a good many regrets. To have his two sons present on his 60th birthday, therefore, must have been a poignant reminder to him, that although he had failed us, we were apparently pulling through. Colin and I both bought him very special gifts, which he was absolutely thrilled with, and he was really pleased to have us around. He made quite an effort to respond to us too, which he didn't always do, and to try and make sure that we enjoyed it as much as he did. It is one of the happiest times that I ever spent with him.

Less than a year later, he was dead. He had suffered a stroke whilst parking his car in the garage one day, and as he slumped over the steering wheel in a coma, a neighbour was alerted by the continual blast of the horn. The ambulance rushed him to hospital, where he lasted about six weeks. It was the second time in his life that he'd had a stroke, but on the first occasion had made a complete recovery. This time things were different. I knew that he was going to die, and when Mr King called me to one side after school one day, it was not difficult to guess what he was going to say. It didn't make it any easier though, and when he actually imparted the news as gently as he could, I just stood rooted to the spot. I could feel the tears coming and I had to be alone.

I walked out of the Colt House and into the grounds, fighting back the tears as I went. I just couldn't let my feelings go. It was too painful. I walked blindly for about an hour in the Deer Park in a state of numbness. Then a sudden burst of anger bore up inside me like a volcano. I mentally shook my fist at fate and wondered "Why. Why pile on one agony after another? Hadn't I suffered enough misery in my life already? The question stared me starkly in the face and remained completely unanswered. I kept walking. I looked at the trees and the sky and felt that even they could not afford me any solace now.

I arrived back at the Colt House, still in a state of numbed disbelief. I could not resolve the whole thing in my mind that quickly. Maybe in time I could learn to accept it, but what of now? Right now, I had to appear before other people, to react in a normal way and take part in the daily routine. How were they to know that things were any different? They couldn't see my pain and desolation. From the outside, I must have looked exactly the same. No, I felt that if I was to survive, I had to crush my feelings, to stamp them out and pretend that they didn't exist.

Fortunately, however, these feelings of anger and emotional repression were short lived.

The news of my father's illness took place during the summer holiday of 1968. Six months prior to this my mother had been admitted to mental hospital for the second time, having suffered another nervous breakdown. Life for me was getting worse all the time. I still had a problem with my holidays too, and each time the end of term drew near, I used to dread the upheaval of having to try and sort out with the staff and the children's department exactly where I was going to stay for that particular holiday. The summer holidays were the worst as it always meant moving between four or five different places. I hated it. I felt like a useless piece of luggage that had to be deposited somewhere for six weeks and it was just a question of which locker they were going to slot me into and when.

Thankfully there were exceptions to this, the most notable being a camping holiday in France. This was being organised for myself and my brother Colin, by Simon Rodway. Also included was my friend from Lacton Hall, who had Simon as his CCO. Simon was really beginning to become a sort of lifeline to me at this point. Here was someone who took an interest in my life and always responded in a positive way, without being in a direct position of authority. He had a good deal to do with Colin and the connection to my life was on a much more relaxed one-to-one basis than was my relationship with any of the staff at Caldecott. In a sense, he was becoming a source of emotional support for me, however tenuous it may have been at that stage. The main point was, that I knew he was always there in the background, and although not wholly connected with the mess that was my life, was at least available if needed.

It was a great shame, that the holiday in France had to be overshadowed by my father's illness. Having had the stroke, he was admitted, ironically, into the cottage hospital which his great grandfather had been instrumental in setting up so many years earlier. However, the facilities there were not sufficient to meet the needs of someone in his condition and before long he was moved to Southampton General Hospital, which was much more modern.

After careful discussion, we decided that we would still go on a holiday, but that we would call in and see him on the way over to France, and then maintain daily phone contact with the hospital once we were there. On the way over, he didn't seem too bad, all things considered, and that helped to put our minds at rest.

We then set about trying to enjoy the holiday. It was a great thrill for me to be going abroad for the first time, I kept thinking to myself how strange it would feel to actually walk on foreign soil! When we finally arrived and drove off the ferry, I was mildly surprised to find that it was not so different from England after all! We put up in a hotel, which was another interesting experience for me and really very exciting.

The next day we drove to our campsite in Brittany and pitched tents. It was great to explore a totally different environment, to go in French cafes and practice my schoolboy French. On the whole, we had some laughs and it was a good holiday, but always in the back of my mind was my father lying in his hospital bed. Simon and Colin would talk about the fact that if he recovered, he might be paralysed down one side, be unable to speak properly, or both. This was very distressing for me, and I couldn't stand the thought of seeing him like that.

For a while it seemed that he was staging a recovery. I began to feel relieved. Then one evening after the call to England, Simon told us that he had taken a turn for the worse and felt that we should go back immediately. I began to grow fearful and panic stricken, sensing that his death could not be far off. Simon, obviously realising the effect the news had on me, took me to one side and we walked a few hundred yards across a stubble field that was our campsite. It was early evening, the sun was low in the sky and it was just the kind of beautiful setting that I could really have appreciated had it been in happier circumstances. As it was, he talked sympathetically about the situation, and at one point put his arm round my shoulder. I can't remember exactly what he said, but for a few brief moments it helped ease the pain and for a while at least, made it easier to accept.

Then we arrived back in England. When we got to my father's bedside, he was half sitting up with pillows behind him to prop him up. He knew who we were, even though he rambled on incoherently most of the time. He took Colin's hand and then mine. As he squeezed it tightly, I could sense that he was trying to say something, but his face could only register the pain and frustration at not being able to do so. At times he talked of our futures and whilst I could not pinpoint the exact thought processes, he was obviously desperately keen that we should make a success of our lives. He had in the past, often said to Colin, you will look after little Tony, won't you? I knew that I couldn't bear it if he died, but when I left his hospital bed that day, it was the last time I ever saw him.

Chapter 24
Funeral

I then returned to Caldecott for the winter term. It was only a couple of weeks before the news of his death came through and after the initial shock came the funeral. In order to attend this, I took a train up to London and stayed the night with Colin at Simon's flat. Simon had decided to come to the funeral with us and the next morning we all set off. It was about 45 miles from London to the Church where the funeral was being held, and despite leaving in good time, the traffic was so bad, that we realised before long that we were going to be late.

The very thought of missing even a part of the funeral, was just too awful to contemplate. It would have been a sickening irony and as the minutes passed, a feeling of nausea temporarily took over my feelings of grief and I sat mentally counting each minute as we dodged in and out of the oncoming traffic. Colin was driving and obviously growing more and more anxious too. He began to take ever greater risks when overtaking, which only added to the stress. Some 3 miles away from the church, Colin inadvertently cut up another driver, in a desperate bid to miss an oncoming lorry.

Fortunately, an accident was narrowly averted. However, the driver of the other car was furious and started to chase us, with the obvious intention of having a row when he caught up with us. The pressure was unbelievable. Finally, we arrived at the church just as the coffin was being carried in.

As we pulled up and got out, the other car skidded to a halt behind us. The driver scrambled out and began advancing rapidly towards Colin, saying "What the hell do you think your game is?" Or words to that effect and was obviously preparing for a showdown. Had Simon not intervened at that moment, a scuffle would almost certainly have taken place. As it was, he leapt out of the car, rushed around to the irate driver and said, "For pity's sake leave him alone, can't you see he's about to attend his father's funeral?" and indicated the coffin entering the church. The flabbergasted driver took one look at the assembled mourners, gave an embarrassed mumble of an apology and hastily beat a retreat.

Heaving an inward sigh of relief, we braced ourselves and walked hurriedly across to the church. As we joined the tail end of the mourners, a few startled, almost disapproving looks, were cast in our direction and we were thrust forward as unobtrusively as possible to a pew near the front. We took our places and sat in a silent state of tense expectancy. I cast my eyes around the church, glossing over the other mourners as they either knelt and prayed or just sat silent and subdued. Then my eyes alighted upon the Coffin, laid out in front of the altar for all to see, and it served only to reinforce my deep feelings of loss.

After the service was over, we followed the coffin back up the aisle, and walked to the graveside. After it had been lowered into the grave and committal had taken place, we walked slowly and painfully away. Then, quite unexpectedly, my aunt Evelyn offered me a few words of comfort and I felt closer to her that moment than I'd ever done before, or indeed since.

The gathering afterwards for tea and sandwiches at my uncle Harry's house was awful. I couldn't understand how people could eat and drink normally as though nothing had happened. There they all were, talking in everyday terms, eating sandwiches and once or twice subdued laughter would ripple across the room. In hindsight, of course, this is just a normal state of affairs after any funeral, but for me at 15 years old, it was inconceivable, for my world had just been shattered for the umpteenth time.

Chapter 25
Leaving

When I returned to Caldecott after the funeral, it was a sharp reminder of the stark reality that lay before me, which I now had to try and adjust to even though it increasingly meant very little to me. Life became a kind of frustrating monotony, with only the occasional high spots. Feelings of depression set in and these depressions would last for several days at a time. I would sometimes go off on my own in the evenings and could be very uncommunicative and offhand with my friends. As a result of this, I began to grow away from the other children all around me, as half the time I was too depressed to even feel like mixing with them, and when I did, I found that I couldn't very well anyway.

Life for them was becoming more sophisticated, and any confidence that I developed in my early years at Caldecott was rapidly waning. The effects of my very early life when I had hardly mixed with other children at all, was beginning to take its toll. I was at the age when people are most self-conscious anyway, and on top of that my insight had developed enough to show me that I had failings in that area. This feeling of isolation and being left behind socially, was enhanced by the dual factor of going out to a school where, at that stage, I was the only Caldecott boy present and secondly, by finding that even when I was back at Caldecott, the two friends I was closest to from Lacton Hall and the Paddocks, quite naturally were tending to spend more time with other boys, as a result of mixing with them all day at school.

All of these feelings were suddenly and rather drastically brought to a head in me when, on one occasion, to try and escape from the situation I found myself in, I bought a bottle of wine and drank it down in large gulps. It wasn't long before my senses began to reel in a rather unpleasant fashion and I lurched towards the Colt House in a rather ungainly manner.

As I walked inside, it became obvious, fairly quickly to all present, that I was exceedingly drunk. One of the boys pointed this out to me in a rather jokey manner, being unaware that I was in a slightly unhinged state of mind. I reacted to this by taking a swing at him, but in my inebriated state, lacked the coordination to do this properly. He ducked and neatly missed my cumbersome blow and as a result I overbalanced and fell across the table tennis table. This greatly amused one of the other boys, who either laughed or made some sort of derisory comment as to my plight. A few seconds later he probably wished that he hadn't. I regained my balance, turned around and punched him straight in the face. The impact of the blow sent him sprawling across a desk behind him, and I then lurched off once more, tripped and fell flat on my face.

By that time, word had spread very rapidly around the Colt House that I was not only drunk, but was in a very violent and aggressive state too. Two or three of my friends arrived on the scene and tried to calm me down. They warned me that if I didn't, I would be in real trouble. I just ignored their advice and hurled abuse at them. I then tried to push my way through them in order to go outside again. They resisted me, however, and a long struggle ensued as they tried to overpower me. I fought like mad and lashed out with punches and kicks in all directions until they finally managed to gain control of the situation and proceeded to drag me to my room. Once there, they heaved me onto my bed and sat on top of me so that I couldn't move. Eventually, I calmed down.

The next morning, I woke up, amazingly enough, without a hangover. I did have a fat lip though, which I had acquired because of falling flat on my face the night before. All my friends were relatively goodhearted about the incident and I apologised to the boy whom I had punched in the face. When I arrived at school, a few of my mates asked me what I'd been up to the night before and I just told them that I'd fallen over and cut my lip. When I got back from school that evening and had eaten my tea, the man who ran the Colt House called me to one side for the "official inquest".

He asked me where I got the wine and why I had done it. To his great credit, he was trying to handle the situation with kindness and empathy, but I didn't respond. I was just too angry and too screwed up inside to care. I just wanted to get it over with. He continued to probe me with questions about some potato wine that I had made, thinking that I had got drunk on that. "You'll have to tip it away now, you know", he said, "I can't risk having you drunk again".

He then asked me for reassurance and an undertaking that I wouldn't do it again, saying that it had caused a great deal of upset for everyone. I as good as told him that it was too bad and that I might well do it again if I felt like it. This just made him angry and eventually he gave up on me and told me that I would have to do a 'Penalty Run'. To make him angrier still, I asked if that meant that I would lose my PU into the bargain. He stared at me incredulously and bellowed, "Of course it means you lose your PU" and stormed off out of the room. That was the first of many occasions in which I indulged in alcohol in subsequent years, in order to try and relieve my inner turbulence and frustrations.

Venom

That bitter mixture of
pain, poison and pus.

Festering, deep down inside.
Just waiting to be hurled
at some unsuspecting
individual.

Who knows where it comes from?

Seek me, seek my past, it says,
and I will show you.

By this time, I was in an almost totally negative and self-destructive frame of mind. The act of getting drunk as far as I was concerned, was not only to relieve my immediate feelings of anger and frustration, but also, I consider in retrospect, as a kind of plea for help. It was a classic case of "Not waving, but drowning", but no-one appeared to notice. It may be that no-one could have helped me at that stage. I do not know. They could have tried though, that was the point. They could have referred me to a psychotherapist, they could have tried talking to me, they could have done anything to show me they could see that I was in pain, but they didn't.

Whatever the reason, it seemed that they were abandoning me in my hour of greatest need. Thus, in what became a rather skewed vision of my life and my relationship with the staff at Caldecott, I felt that the people I had come to depend on, who had helped me through so much in the past, and had restored some my faith in human race, were now deserting me. It was like being in a huge fish tank and not being able to swim.

Looking back, I can't really blame them. I believe they did the best they could with the resources that were available to them at the time.

Nonetheless, I still had a couple of terms to go before leaving, which I perceived as being two terms of living with the same boring routine of going to school every day and taking, what I then saw as stupid, pointless exams. It all seemed so meaningless. Staff wanted me to stay another year after that and take O-levels, but there was no way that I was going to do that. They also tried to encourage me to think about a career, so I half-heartedly thought about entering the civil service, took the entrance exam and failed. Any ideas of jobs were really only done in response to promptings by James King and others and my attitude towards it all was really very limp.

My anger against the staff continued to grow and I felt that if they were not going to help me, then they must expect to get kicked in the teeth. So, to my great shame, I made a point of screwing up the staff in whatever way I could, however small the gesture. I would often argue with the man who was now running the Colt House just for the hell of it, always waiting for a chance to prove him wrong and humiliate him. It became a kind of obsession with me to do things that I knew would upset him and the other staff too, if at all possible. He probably began to despise me for it, but I didn't care.

It was at this time that the idea of taking drugs began to take shape in my mind. Apart from natural curiosity to see what they were like I was subconsciously using the idea as a kind of weapon to get back at the staff and the world in general. I was aware that people could die from an overdose of certain drugs, but not of the dreadful effects they can have on people's minds. There was also, of course, the kind of nauseating glamour attached to them, which is a terrible travesty. So, in my somewhat wild, naive and self-pitying state, I thought that if I go and kill myself on drugs when I left Caldecott, it would be their fault. It would make them feel guilt and remorse, which was all they deserved. This thought offered me a kind of perverse satisfaction and I resolved to start taking drugs at the earliest possible opportunity upon leaving Caldecott.

As the weeks went by, however, my anger tended to dissipate more into periods of apathy, which became more frequent. I could hardly be bothered after a while to feel angry and try to hit back at the staff.

Finally, my last term arrived, and I took my CSE exams and left school six weeks before the end of term. This gave me a kind of illusory sense of freedom. No more school. I was going to work in the kitchen garden and earn some extra pocket money and it was a great summer weatherwise. What is more, I was practically being treated on an adult status. The staff weren't really too bothered about what I did anymore.

The worst part about the last term for me, was having to make arrangements for a job and accommodation when I left. That was reality. I was just not interested in reality. Why should I go and get a job outside? What was the point? Mr King suggested that I could go to a hostel in London. He was still keen for me to do my O-levels and wondered if I'd like to attend a college in London to do them. This idea did not appeal to me. He did give me the name and address of a hostel there, and suggested I write to them to find out the details of the accommodation and whether they would have me.

I was beginning to get cold feet. The day of reckoning was drawing ever nearer. What would life be like out there? Perhaps I had made a mistake by being so determined to leave Caldecott. It all seemed signed and sealed now though, and the wheels were already in motion. There was no going back at this stage. Paranoia began to set in. It seemed like they were shoving me out, although this was clearly contrary to the truth.

I hadn't bothered to write to the hostel, much to James King's annoyance and frustration and in the event, he arranged for me to have a shared room in a TOC-H Hostel in Tower Hill in London. At that time in its history Caldecott did not provide any real support for children when they left and I was ill-equipped to deal with life in the outside world.

James King had once said to me in a general conversation about life, that we all have to believe in something. The implication being that if we don't, then we have no aims and no purpose in life. By the time I left Caldecott, I didn't really believe in anything at all.

WINTER

Winter

At night I gaze up
into the endless heavens,
losing myself
in the starlit sky.

Cold, dark, isolation.

Only one step from oblivion.

Chapter 26
Toc H

It had already been arranged that I should have my six-week school holiday before taking up a job in September and two weeks of this were taken up with a holiday in a rented cottage in Cornwall. This was with Simon Rodway, my brother Colin, and my Paddocks and Lacton Hall friend. This proved to be a most enjoyable and welcome break with very good weather. For the rest of the time, I was staying at the Toc H hostel in London and looking for a job.

During my holiday period I was given an assortment of rooms to stay in and not allotted a permanent one until September. Nearly all the rooms at Toc H were shared and mine was no exception. The first person I shared with was a man in his early 20s who had only recently come to England. I think he was studying and needed peace and quiet to do that. For me the idea of having to share a room with somebody even a stranger, did not strike me as being at all unusual as I been used to freely mixing in this way at Caldecott.

During my holiday I had registered with an employment agency and tried to obtain some form of employment. My brother had entered the field of insurance and seem to be quite enjoying it and making good progress in his career. However, as I almost totally lacked ambition of any sort, the idea that any job could be either satisfying or fulfilling, was completely alien to me. I therefore got a job as a labourer in a wine cellar. This basically consisted of being part of a four-man team in the bottling shop and carrying out very routine functions such as corking bottles, placing plastic caps on them and storing them in their appropriate racks and so on. This was rather soul-destroying and the only positive aspects as far as I was concerned was the easy company of the other men there, which at times could be quite fun and there was also the chance of drinking free booze!

Although I enjoyed certain aspects of the camaraderie of my newfound friends, such as the jokes, the drinking, the playing cards and general horseplay, there was always the underlying belief that I began to develop, that there had to be more to life than this. As it happens, there was another young man there of about my age, also called Tony, who had long hair, liked progressive music and played the drums in his own rock band. This was only a part-time venture however, and they mainly just played around pubs in the East End.

At this stage, I was growing my hair ever longer wearing more "Way Out" clothes and was just beginning to develop a taste for progressive rock music. I had bought a record player during the holiday and from the £10 a week I was earning at the wine cellar I could afford to buy an LP every so often having paid the rent, which included food. I still had enough left over to buy cigarettes and the odd pint of beer at the pub. Occasionally I would overspend and have to get a sub from the company until payday. Thus, my collection of LPs began to grow gradually, some of them purchased on the advice of my drummer friend in the wine cellar.

One evening Tony and his band were practising somewhere in the East End and he and invited me along. After work I went back to his house and met some of his mates and we drove around in their van collecting everyone's equipment. They each had their respective girlfriends with them. When they arrived at the practice venue and set up their equipment, they duly blasted out a few numbers and were reasonably competent, if not a particularly inspiring band. I quite enjoyed the music, but to some extent felt a bit out of my depth, as I wasn't sure exactly how I should conduct myself in this situation.

Back in the hostel, apart from scant contact with the other residents, I didn't socialise with them at all. For me it was not a natural thing to do and was a somewhat peculiar notion.

Fortunately, however, I did get visits from Simon and my brother Colin, whilst at Toc H, as well as my friends from Caldecott, John and Chris. These provided me with a certain stability and a sense of belonging whilst they took place, but in the periods in between, I experienced more of the depression that I began to have during my last year Caldecott. So, I tended to turn to drink and music, in order to keep going. A number of my evenings at Toc H, as a result of this, were spent, after mealtimes at any rate, just lying on my bed with a supply of beer and listening to such music as Cream, John Mayall's Blues Breakers, Canned Heat, the Beatles and other similar music that I had at the time.

The one positive activity that I indulged in at this stage, however, was that of playing the guitar. Having started in a very minor way at the Colt House by learning one or two chords, I later bought a second-hand guitar from John, purchased a few books illustrating chords and fingerpicking styles and with his occasional tuition on visits, set about improving my standard of play. My enthusiasm for this project was actually very strong and I made myself practice on a regular basis and I soon became reasonably proficient. Over the ensuing year or so, my guitar playing became a very important part of my life and I managed to gain a fairly high degree of satisfaction from it.

After a couple of months my roommate asked to be transferred to another room. This was probably due partly to the music that I played and partly, I suspect, that he found my company to be rather depressing. For a while I had the room to myself, which actually suited me better, until another young man of about 25 came to the hostel and moved into my room with me. I slightly resented this intrusion at first but soon grew used to it, particularly as this man was a very nice person. He was an up-and-coming photographer by profession and had a very busy social life in connection with this. He also fitted in very well with the younger section of the office workers at the hostel, but I continued to prefer to drink on my own in my room for much of the time and listen to records.

After a while, my new roommate must also have got rather fed up with sharing a room with a very morose young man, who appeared to make no effort whatsoever to go out and make friends and he obviously felt that I was a bit of a jerk. One evening when he arrived back late and I was three parts drunk he more or less told me this, saying that I ought to stop moping around, pull myself together and go out and make some friends and enjoy myself.

In one sense he was perfectly right of course, as lying around drinking and listening to records every evening is hardly the best way for anyone, let alone a 17-year-old to spend his time. However, I just couldn't see how to relate to other people. I still didn't understand the dynamics of what was involved in personal relationships. I was able to make easy superficial interaction in environments where I had to, such as at work, but could not translate that into purely social situations. I think subconsciously a part of me may have wanted to go and enjoy myself, make friends of both sexes and be happy, but clearly this was not going to happen.

The realisation at this point of seeing for the first time an aspect of my personality as other people saw it, served only to heighten my resentment against life and made me feel even more of a social outcast. I couldn't face up to this, so I began to step up my drinking habits. However, as I was very short of money, I had to resort to stealing the odd bottle of whiskey from the wine cellar where I worked, either for consumption by myself, or to sell cheaply to other people in the hostel. At the same time, I was regularly taking out subs each week from the company and buying drink from them on credit.

In the meantime, although life in the wine cellar was boring workwise, it was still relatively enjoyable in terms of the easy and undemanding mateyness that prevailed there. During the run-up to Christmas that year, there was much in the way of overtime to be done and although very hard work, it was worth it in terms of the extra money involved. I also had the chance to accompany one of the van drivers on some of his rounds and received several generous tips from the customers.

Christmas Day and Boxing Day that year were spent in Simon's flat and although he had gone to spend Christmas with his mother in the country, Colin and I had our mother over to spend it with us. These two days proved to be an oasis of family warmth and blessing and for a brief spell lifted me out of the uncomfortable reality of the life that lay before me.

After that it was back to life as usual at Toc H and the wine cellar and I was beginning to find the job rather too much. During one or two of the recent visits from John and Chris, we had discussed the possibility of getting a small flat together down in Kent near to where John worked. He was happy in his job was about to complete his apprenticeship and therefore had no desire to leave it. Chris, on the other hand, having joined the police cadets was finding it most unsuitable for him and didn't wish to join the police after his training period finished. I, of course, was only too pleased to have the chance of leaving my job and quitting the hostel, which although essentially a very good one, was not suitable for me. We therefore decided as soon as possible that we would find a flat near John's place of work, which was also near to Caldecott and that Chris and I would find jobs nearby too.

After a while I grew impatient at waiting, was sick to death of my job and decided upon getting up one morning, to pack my bags and leave both job and hostel. This I did, leaving behind a small debt to the wine company and a rather bigger one to the hostel. I duly headed in the direction of Caldecott, hoping that they would put me up until I could find a flat.

During the last year or so of my time in the Colt House, there was a Dutch woman in her early 20s whose job was to help out in the pantry and kitchen. She was very vivacious and good looking and a number of us Colt House boys were attracted to her. I had got quite friendly with her and during my stay at Toc H, I maintained contact by letter and always eagerly awaited hers to me. She had given me one of her neck scarves, which still faintly retained the scent she used and I wore it a lot. Once or twice during this period when I visited Caldecott, I would spend a little time with her when I could. On one occasion when we were alone, we went to bed, but nothing came of it.

On the School Steps

There they were.
He, hands on hips,
posing.
She 23, mini-skirted,
and smiling.

And me, 16, looking on,
less confident
of her affections
and desiring
a pure love.

Strange how this
black and white photo
radiates
such colourful memories
of the "Summer of 69".

A spring awakening,
killed by unexpected frost.

All so distant now,
but funny how things
can catch you.... unawares.

Chapter 27
Back to Caldecott

When I arrived back at Caldecott and explained to Mr King that I'd left both job and hostel, he was none too pleased and told me, with a slight sense of urgency, that I could stay at Caldecott for the time being until I got fixed up. However, he was obviously worried that I might be a bad influence on the other children with my drinking habits and general negative outlook.

Oddly, I was quite pleased to be back in the safe familiar environment of Caldecott, despite my extreme negativity towards it when I left. However, it also hit home rather hard that I did not belong to the place anymore and I found this rather difficult to accept.

Although Caldecott provided on the whole a very good standard of care for all the children that passed through it, the after-care at that stage was minimal and I was all at sea and needed somewhere that I could call home. They did to their credit, put me up in rather difficult circumstances, but I still felt a bit like an intruder and unwanted guest. This lack of after-care is a major fault for any residential home for children that substantially abandons them at the end of their stay without providing any intermediate support in order to help them adjust to life in the outside world.

Thus, having thrust myself upon them, they provided accommodation for me whilst I looked around for a flat and a job in the locality. In the meantime, I spent some of my evenings down at the local pub with John and one or two of his mates and the Dutch woman and her friend. I soon realised that the woman I was so keen on was actually going strong with one of John's friends and found this very upsetting. This was because I knew that John's friend was obviously being successful where I had failed so dismally a few months earlier.

I began to feel increasingly resentful as the evening went on and got progressively more drunk. At closing time, we all wandered back to Caldecott together, except for John's friend who had to get back that night and couldn't stay around. I was very glad about this and when we got back to the little Bothy, where the Dutch women stayed, we went in for a few more drinks and played some records.

Before very long, however, something that either she, or somebody said, triggered off in me a sudden feeling of animosity towards her and in a fit of rage I stood up and started shouting and pushing things over in her room and then, whilst yelling abuse at her, took hold of one of her dresses and tore it in half. She then burst into floods of tears and started shouting insults back at me.

This situation seemed continue for some time until eventually I went outside only to find that Mr King had been called over from the main house in order to take charge of the situation. Upon seeing my condition, he told me that he was going to take me to hospital to have my stomach pumped out. I didn't take to this idea very much and a struggle ensued, with Mr King and one or two others trying to bundle me into the school car and take me to hospital. After a few minutes they succeeded and I calmed down during the drive to the hospital.

When we arrived though, the idea of the stomach pump proved to be too much for me and I started struggling again, so much so that the police were called and finally after much scuffling and abuse hurled at all and sundry, I was finally overpowered and held down whilst a stomach pump was administered in order to make me vomit all of the alcohol that I had consumed. After this process had been carried out, I was taken to the local police station and spent the night sleeping it off in a cell. During the night I was sick once again and one of the policemen stood over me while I cleared it up and I then went back to sleep once more.

The next morning at about 6 am. I was woken up and taken along to the charge room and formally charged with being drunk and disorderly. I was then handed back my possessions and told to make my own way back to Caldecott. I told them that I didn't have any money for the bus fare and asked them to give me a lift back. They refused point blank of course and told me that I would have to walk. I then wearily embarked on the trek back to Caldecott and arrived at about 7am. with nobody apparently having stirred, feeling very hung over, a little disorientated and very slightly ashamed.

There was no real inquest from Mr King or anyone else for that matter regarding my behaviour, largely I suppose, as I was no longer under their jurisdiction. This feeling of there being no form of retribution coming to me from Caldecott, as it certainly would have been eight months earlier, left me with a strange, empty feeling, which was heightened by the rather frosty reception that I received from all the staff during the next few days. It was almost as if I didn't exist for them anymore and isolation once again began to crowd around me like a cold, heavy overcoat.

A short while afterwards, I had to attend court and after a brief appearance before the magistrate during which I apologised for my actions, I was fined £5 (half a week's wages in those days) and that was that. In the meantime, John, Chris and I found a little flat in a small village nearby and we duly moved in and took up residence.

Chapter 28
Village Life!

This flat was part of a rather dilapidated, dirty old house, which had formerly been a hotel and had since been converted into about five separate flatlets. However, in spite of its condition, we took it and were very pleased to have our own flat together and prepared to start enjoying life.

Having got the flat, the next step was to find a job in order to pay the rent and buy food and other necessities. John, who was in employment, put up the initial money for the deposit and advance rent as Chris and I started to look around for jobs. We looked at a variety of very un-interesting ones and finally landed up by taking jobs as labourers in an iron foundry. The wages for this job were in the region of £10 a week and the work was hard physical labour in a hot, dusty, and very noisy environment. I did not readily take to it, but it did at least provide an income of some sort, so it was at least tolerable in that it provided for me during my leisure hours.

These were mainly taken up with going to the pub, playing records or continuing to play the guitar, which I had been busily learning at Toc H. I was now getting to the stage where I could compose my own little songs and instrumentals and this gave me a great deal of satisfaction and pleasure. John, who had been playing the guitar for some years was very competent and a source of inspiration to both Chris and me. I also became interested in the folk songs of Mississippi John Hurt, a singer re-discovered in the mid-60s at the Newport Folk Festival. Also, another singer called Blind Lemon Jefferson who performed his special brand of blues around the Chicago area in the 1920s. We sought to imitate their finger picking styles, which was a very enjoyable challenge.

Life at this stage jogged on quite happily for a while, but soon the novelty of having the flat began to wear off and the routine of going to work every day, spending seven hours doing such a dull and onerous job, made life seem rather less exciting. Apart from this, we were all beginning to quarrel over ridiculous things and we started to feel slightly antagonistic towards each other at times. Chris and John were beginning to conduct their own social lives too, which for John was merely the continuation of what he been doing anyway. So, I began once again to feel left out.

This brought back my feelings of depression again, which had largely abated for several months and I began to search around in my mind for a way out of this situation.

As sometimes happens, fate stepped in at this point in the form of two weeks notice from the landlady, who told us that we must go as we were not suitable tenants. We were absolutely staggered about this, particularly as our conduct, on the whole, had been very acceptable by normal social standards and nothing that we had done warranted our being thrown out. The only factor that may have influenced the landlady's thinking was that two of us had long hair and scruffy clothes. At this period in the late 60s and early 70s this was an automatic passport being condemned as being a thoroughly useless, undesirable layabout.

After a few days, however, we began slowly to accept the situation as a fete accompli and without realising, or even caring at that stage that we could have taken her to court for her actions, began to think about making alternative arrangements. As far as I was concerned, going back to Caldecott, even temporarily, was out of the question. For obvious reasons I was less than enamoured of the place at the time and almost certainly they with me.

The only other place in the world that I could go to at that point, was to Simon's flat in London and stay with him and my brother Colin, at least until I could find my own room and a job. So having spent about six months with Chris and John in the flat, in October 1970 I was back off to London for a second try at making a go of things on my own. I left behind a couple of friends who were both carving out their own little niche in life and one in which I could play no part.

I had thus arrived at a point, where, my isolation, my awareness of my inability to relate satisfactorily with other people and the unhappiness that I was experiencing a result, left me facing a kind of mental blank wall. I began to think that there must be something of value in life, or some meaning. Surely it couldn't just consist of this vacuum or emptiness. So, I started subconsciously seeking something to redress the balance, something to give me hope.

I came to believe increasingly, that I must eventually find happiness and satisfaction somewhere and ultimately find life more fulfilling. I wasn't searching for this in a religious sense and indeed could not have formulated my thoughts about it in this way, but it was just a kind of inner conviction. Neither was I looking for a mystical experience of any sort, but just something that would give me a sense of purpose. So, in this mixed emotional state, I arrived back in London at Simon's flat.

Chapter 29
Kaleidoscope

Having arrived back in London, I felt happy initially at being in the flat with Colin and Simon, albeit temporarily. My first task was to find both a room and a job, which with long hair and scruffy clothes was not an easy one. I completely refused, however, to change my appearance and instead enlisted the help of my mother in searching for a room, as she would lend an air of respectability to a potential landlord. She lived nearby and was very willing to help me in this way and fortunately before long we found a nice room which I was really pleased about. The landlord appeared to be a very reasonable sort of person who was obviously quite prepared to have a tenant as scruffy as I was in one of his properties. He actually had a bigger house elsewhere and every week I was to call round and pay one weeks rent in advance.

Having got my room and moved in, I had to get a job and having registered with a couple of agencies got one with a wholesale company in the city packing calendars and diaries. Everything so far seem to be progressing in a satisfactory manner and this proved to be even more so when I discovered that there was another young man of my age with long hair who worked for this company also. His name was Paul and before long I struck up a friendship with him. He had come down from Manchester about six months previously, having got fed up with living at home with his parents and got himself a large room in Hammersmith. He shared this with a friend of his, who had also come down to London with him for the same reason.

After chatting with him and finding that we both like the same sort of music he asked me if I smoked dope. I replied that I hadn't done so yet, as I hadn't known where to get hold of any but was most anxious to try it. He then invited me round to his place that evening as he had just got himself a supply.

When evening came round, I accompanied him on the tube back to his place, met his friend and having all had a meal of fish and chips, Paul rolled a joint. We passed it round and then just sat back and listened to various records like Hendrix and Led Zeppelin. The first few occasions that I smoked it, it did not appear to have very much affect, but certainly made me feel very pleasant and relaxed.

My friendship with Paul continued and apart from spending quite a few evenings and weekends with him, during which he introduced me to others of his friends, we regularly smoked a variety of dope. Of all these, the one that had the most effect on me was Marijuana or "Grass". Being stronger, it was sometimes possible to hallucinate in a mild way, especially when listening to music and it seemed to heighten the senses. It also tended to remove inhibitions and heighten sexual desire. In my case, however, this last category was totally unfulfilled, unlike my friends around me who were regularly indulging their desires as they pleased. So, I began to push this aspect of things into the background, thinking that as I had got such problems in this area, this whole part of my personality was best ignored. Instead, I felt that I got a lot of stimulation in other ways, namely listening to many and varied forms of rock music, which under the influence of Marijuana sounded incredible.

So, apart from The Who, Pink Floyd, Hendrix and so on, I was introduced to other bands such as The Doors, Jethro Tull, Ten Years After, CSN&Y and Spirit, with their weird album "The 12 Dreams of Dr. Sardonicus". One, which had particular resonance for me, was Keef Hartley's band. On the album, "Half Breed", the track "Born to Die" with its brilliant guitar solo really reflected the mental state that I sporadically experienced.

Also at this time, I first became aware of the so-called "Revolution" that was taking place. This was largely through reading such magazines as "IT and "OZ". These underground papers were an extraordinary mixture of serious political comment and articles on the state of the "Establishment", through to news and reports on rock music and the new youth culture. They also contained cartoons of men and women of a grossly exaggerated sexual nature. Subjects such as the now predictable sex, drugs and rock'n'roll, tended to dominate these papers, but there were also other ideas and letters too, about what direction the so-called "Revolution" was heading in and whether or not this was to be a purely political revolution, or whether it meant just changing people's attitudes or what.

I found all of these new ideas and experiences fascinating, but also very confusing. I also began to feel that I was becoming a part of this "Revolution" that appeared to be taking place, without really knowing how or why. At the same time a part of me was beginning to turn against the so-called "straight establishment" (by which I mean conventional, not "straight" in the sense of gay or straight). This was really made up of anyone who either didn't take drugs and have long hair, or who had no understanding or empathy with the social upheaval that was taking place.

As far as the political aspect of all this was concerned, capitalism was rejected by the new culture, as being purely the means by which a handful of unscrupulous people were exploiting the majority of the nation's workforce in order to make as much profit out of it as possible for themselves. Thus, they were not serving the best interests of all the people. The police a.k.a. "the pigs" the "straight press" and the Judges, were all held in the highest contempt as well, being perceived as merely the corrupt instruments of state whose sole reason for existing was to serve the evil capitalist masters. This basically meant screwing down everyone else for their benefit and imposing unnecessary laws that restricted freedom, such as the freedom to take recreational drugs. Now whilst there was undoubtedly some truth in certain aspects of all this, much of it was wildly exaggerated.

So, what with my growing awareness, not just politically, but culturally too, it became more and more apparent that the new culture was totally rejecting the straight establishment and vice versa. Without really grasping all of what was taking place, I readily identified myself with this new culture and immediately adopted all of their ideas into my sphere of thinking.

Of the many other aspects of this so-called revolution that was taking place, there was the desire to get back to nature, bringing with it the belief that civilisation had gone too far technologically for its own good and was thus destroying the earth ecologically speaking and squandering its resources. This was taking place by mass-producing many products which humanity had no real need of anyway. So, this period really became the birth of the ecology movement and ultimately the inception of the Green Party. There were also the anti-Vietnam war demonstrations and, in the USA, the Civil Rights marches with Martin Luther King. Just so much was happening. As far as I was concerned, I grappled with this maelstrom of ideas, but it was in a somewhat naïve and gullible way.

Then there were the CND marches against the threat of the growth of nuclear weapons and the possibility of humanity blowing itself to pieces and for what? There was also the pollution of the atmosphere and much of the food that we ate, which gave a huge boost to the consumption of whole foods, in order to better preserve our physical health. Also, yoga and meditation were taken as being very important for physical, mental and spiritual well-being and apart from this there were many new religious cults and spiritual ideas that were springing up all over the place, which meant that almost every aspect of life was undergoing radical change for anyone who chose to become a part of it.

Much of this of course was spawned by people like Allen Ginsberg, Jerry Rubin and Andy Warhol, as well as the Beatles, Bob Dylan and many other bands who communicated it by their words, through their music and to some extent their actions.

The feminist movement gathered pace through the publication of various women's books including Germaine Greer's "The Female Eunuch". This was really the advent of the "Permissive Society", when "doing your own thing" became the norm. Unfortunately, it didn't come with a health warning.

There were also other people around such as the Maharishi and Meher Barber, Tariq Ali and Timothy Leary, all of whom were influencing for good or ill different people in different ways and on different philosophical and spiritual levels. Timothy Leary, in particular, was advocating the widespread use of LSD, almost as a kind of panacea for all that was wrong with the world. I therefore found myself at the age of 17 caught up in this whirlwind of new ideas and theories and changes in attitudes, which was, on the whole, exhilarating, if not rather daunting.

I then began to experiment with LSD or "acid" as it was known. This came about partly through Paul, who was not sure whether he should try it out or not. He obviously felt a little apprehensive as to what the effects might be, having heard a multitude of stories about both the good and bad effects that it can have on people. I was not so cautious at this stage, however, and was willing to plunge into any new experience at the drop of a hat. So, I persuaded him to try some with me. A couple of other guys also decided to come in on it with us and so we called round to the dealer a few streets away and bought a tablet each. Having arrived back at Paul's room, we decided to display at least a little caution and drop only half a "tab" to start with. This we duly did and before very long the effects of the drug started. This first trip seemed fantastic and whilst I was still experiencing it, I took the other half tab to in order to prolong and heighten it as much as possible.

To try and describe the effects of this seductive and pernicious drug is extremely difficult and the results of taking it vary enormously according to both the quality and quantity taken and more important the mood and general mental and emotional condition of the user.

Initially, as I was feeling reasonably satisfied with life at this point, superficially at any rate, the trips that I experienced were good ones. They varied from vaguely mystical to incredibly exciting and exhilarating ones. The hallucinations that I had were quite staggering and even the most mundane surroundings became palaces of the imagination in terms of shapes and colours and sounds.

Even the tiniest objects, could take on vast significance in much the same way that they do with children. Much time could be spent studying the patterns in a carpet or the grain in a piece of wood and watching them change or dance about before your very eyes.

Sometimes it was possible to look at something for several minutes before realising exactly what it was. Virtually anything you imagined you could see, you believed you could actually see. It was almost as if one was entering another dimension in time and space where imagination and reality were one.

After one or two of these trips, I began to understand how some people, presumably after large amounts, had thrown themselves out of windows, believing that they could fly. Such was the extent to which LSD could take over the normal functions of the mind and make things so abstract, that the user could be almost totally removed from reality. Even the traffic in the street outside sounded like music and all sights and sounds were drawn together into a wonderful sort of kaleidoscopic, half dreamlike state, that was capable of producing either wild euphoria, or just as likely, terror into the user.

Drawing pictures or painting under the influence of LSD was quite incredible too, as the shapes and scenes that the hand was capable of depicting were very often astounding. Other people claimed to have actually left their bodies when under the influence, much in the same way that yoga experts in the east claim to do, purely through meditation. On one trip, I was convinced that I was disappearing from other people's sight and momentarily that I had become invisible. Gradually the effects would wear off, however, and leave one with a slight feeling of emptiness, disappointment, and a kind of grey dullness. It also engendered a strong desire for the next trip.

Of the bad trips that I had, unlike some other people, they were not the huge spiders or monsters crawling out of the walls, although once I did have a very rough time whilst watching a horror film on the television. Mine consisted of feelings of ever-increasing paranoia and irrational fears. These fears were mainly those of going mad and losing my mind. Fears of inevitable self-destruction, which made themselves manifest, sometimes in obvious ways like believing that if I stood up and turned off the light the whole room would explode and me with it. Sometimes they were just unspecific fears that hung over me like great black clouds and dominated all my thought processes.

The only way of surviving these bad trips was to tell yourself repeatedly that it wasn't real and that eventually you would come down. Sometimes I wondered if I would actually come down, which only served to increase the intensity of my fears. When other people were on bad trips, they sometimes upset the atmosphere for other people, or created "bad vibes". Somebody would then have to try and talk them down by getting inside the other person's mind as far as possible and steering it in the right direction. Hopefully this would then end the blind panic of the person on the bad trip. As each week went by, all my fears gradually became more and more dominant even permeating my waking life as it were, when I was in between trips.

Many years later I learned that LSD had been invented in the USA as a potential weapon of war and I have seen film of it being experimented on with US soldiers. The authorities soon concluded that even using it in wartime would be immoral, as the effects were so devastating.

Although I was never on drugs for very long and thankfully never took heroin, the devastation was just as bad, due to my extreme mental and emotional condition.

Indeed, if I have one regret in my life it is that of ever taking drugs at all. If I could live my life over again, I wouldn't even have a single puff of Marijuana.

In the meantime, my intense dislike of so-called straight people was developing rapidly all the time, egged on by many of my acquaintances. This, sadly, even came to include to some degree my brother and Simon, who on the one hand I was busily trying to write off because they were "establishment", whilst on the other, I subconsciously knew how badly I needed them.

This feeling of animosity was born very largely as a result of my naive identity with the new culture and the mistaken belief among many people at the time, me included, that the two cultures couldn't mix and learn from each other. I therefore felt that I, too, must reject the old order totally, even though this caused me a considerable amount of pain. This feeling of having to leave the old order behind, was also pushed along unwittingly, because of my newfound association with a couple a few years older than me called Ken and Sheila.

This couple had been living together for a few years and were by and large, nice people. They had left their respective homes as soon as they had been able to and rejected many of the values of their parents and were well into the whole concept of youth culture and revolution. They had been taking drugs for several years, including on the odd occasion mescalin, which is a very powerful form of LSD and were always trying to gain a fuller more complete understanding of life, especially concerning the reasons as to why we are here, where we were heading and also as to how we should conduct ourselves, bearing in mind that we are.

They believed not only in the existence of God, but also a divine master plan that affected not just the earth, but the whole universe. They spoke of different levels of spiritual achievement, believed in reincarnation and a concept known as Karma. This really means anything that we do as human beings, good or bad, eventually comes back on us in one form or another. This is linked with reincarnation too and the idea of learning by one's mistakes and thus evolving spiritually over millions of years. They were very much influenced in this direction by the Beatles and the Maharishi and consequently getting more and more into the idea of religion, particularly that of Hari Krishna.

I much enjoyed their company, almost seeing them as gurus. I used to go and see them quite often and sometimes stay the night. On these occasions I would take trips with them and discuss all of these and other mystical religious topics, which I found challenging.

At the same time, I also became more confused about everything, and it seemed that the further I delved into anything, the more confused I became. My mental perspectives were changing almost daily and I began to become very dependent on any new ideas that they might pass on to me, one such idea was that people shouldn't eat meat. As a result of this before very long I became a complete vegetarian and was always eager to learn and absorb more of the sort of ideas and beliefs that Ken and Sheila held. At one point, I went with them on a visit to the Rhada Krishna temple in central London where they were going to join. I very nearly joined along with them but decided not to at the last minute.

Chapter 30
Apocalypse

It was around this time that I first heard John Lennon's first solo album entitled "Plastic Ono Band, which had just been released. He made this after having had a special form of intense psychoanalysis known as primal therapy. This new form of analysis, as I understand it, had been formulated by a man called Arthur Janov, who believed that it was possible for people to regress mentally to when they were very small, even as far back as when they were born. Having thus got the patient to regress, they would be encouraged to emit what was known as the primal scream and they could then relive their early experiences, good or bad, and come to understand why certain experiences had affected them in certain ways and thus come to terms with their own unhappy or painful feelings.

I'm not entirely certain as to how this worked and how much truth there was in it, but it certainly seemed to help John Lennon and this album was produced as a direct result of it. There was one song on it that hit me right in the solar plexus and kept haunting me for days afterwards. It was called "Mother". For any that don't know this song, it was a kind of eulogy to his lost or substantially non-existent relationship with his mother (and father), as a boy. It was, and still is a most powerful and disturbing song that really affected me, for I could identify his pain with my own. I found it very comforting just to know that somebody, no matter how far removed my own life, had suffered great pain in this way and how it had affected their own outlook and attitudes for years.

Up to that point, I could obviously feel the effects of the prolonged emotional damage that I had sustained and the loneliness it engendered, but hearing that song seemed to validate the hurt and meant that I could now consciously acknowledge it. Although I did not realise it at the time, this was an important first step in bringing healing, although substantial healing didn't take place till many years afterwards.

Then, there was George Harrison's solo album entitled "All things must pass". This was much more spiritually orientated and spoke among other things of the importance of spiritual love and achievement and the forgetting of the self in order to achieve fulfilment and real happiness. It acknowledged God's supremacy and the realisation that we are of infinite value to him. Also the belief that our lives on earth and all earthly things are only temporary.

It also highlighted the importance of giving love as well as receiving love and that God is within all of us if we want him. Further still, it spoke of the way in which we thoughtlessly hurt each other and the many who blindly stumble around feeling lost and unsatisfied. Similarly, how pain and sadness can swallow us up and make us feel bitter and filled with self-pity, which can debilitate our lives.

There was also one song on this album that, again, had a huge impact on me. It was "Run of the Mill", and most significantly the last line which was, "Only you'll arrive at your own made end, with no-one but yourself to be offended. It's you that decides."

All of these ideas from that period continued to have a profound effect on me. Many of them were born out of a desire to improve the lot of the human race and as such were very noble in their conception. There were, however, some philosophies and cults that were inextricably linked in with them which I believe to be of a very dubious nature to say the least. It's also possible that the conditions for the deceptive and often ludicrous conspiracy theories that exist today, could have had their roots in this tumultuous period. These being fuelled by excessive drug use, which, as we know, can cause a whole range of mental health issues. Unfortunately, the internet has lent so much power to these myths. I still believe, however, that some of what came out of the social upheaval that took place during the 60s was positive, despite the bad things, drug abuse being the main one.

Nonetheless, many different types of people were influenced in very many different ways during this period and this slowly permeated our society and brought about change for the better in some, although not all areas.

Thus, whilst I was moving forward mentally in various ways and learning a good deal on the one hand, my practical grip on life was becoming more and more tenuous on the other. This was made manifest by the problems I was about to experience with my accommodation. Having had my room for some two or three months, I found to my great consternation that the landlord had given me four weeks notice to quit as he wanted the house for his daughter. I half-heartedly looked around for alternative accommodation and having been unable to find any after the four weeks had elapsed, came back one day to find my possessions being taken out of my room and placed in the passage by three rather large unpleasant looking men. Protests were useless at this stage and having already asked the landlord for an extension to my notice and been refused, I now turned in desperation to Simon and Colin to help me out of the mess that I was in.

They made arrangements for all my possessions to be brought to the flat and told me that I could stay there until I'd found alternative accommodation. In the meantime, they helped me to take action against the landlord for illegally evicting me. This case was brought against him successfully and he was given quite a heavy fine. In the meantime, I had managed to find another room, again with the help of my mother. This did not last for long, however, as I had now got to the stage where I felt that I did not want to work for a living anymore and as such gave up my job at the calendar wholesalers. I then signed on for unemployment benefit, but as I had given up my job voluntarily, was told that I would not qualify for six weeks. I was able to get some money from Social Security though, which I did, but the amount they gave me was not sufficient for all my needs and as such I was soon unable to pay the rent.

Once again, I was out on the streets and it was down to Simon and Colin to come to my rescue once more. So, after only two months I was back in the flat and sleeping on a camp bed in Colin's room. This situation lasted for several months and must have caused a good deal of disruption in the flat at the time.

During this period, I almost totally went to pieces. I refused to get a job, despite much practical persuasion from both Colin and Simon and all I really wanted to do was to play my guitar and listen to music. Indeed, Colin recorded some of my songs and my guitar playing during this period, which I still have. The flat with Simon and Colin was the one source of warmth and comfort for me during this period, however brief.

Thus, during the weekdays rather than leave me in the flat, they thought that I would be better off out of it. They were probably worried, quite understandably, that if I had free access, I might bring round an assortment of undesirables who might either make a mess of the flat, steal things, or both. In addition to this, they felt that to give me a key would make it seem too much like my own place and they quite rightly wished to foster the idea of it being temporary only.

So, during the day I would just kick up my heels and spent quite a lot of time in libraries. I read a lot of the Sherlock Holmes books at this time and Conan Doyle's short stories. I also spent time going round and round on the underground. One benefit of this was that I got to know the London Underground map extremely well!

After several months of living in the flat, I began to feel sufficiently positive to make the effort to get a job again.

This I did finding a post as a packer for a firm who made reproduction pictures by famous artists. This job suited me quite well at the time and before long I decided that I would move out of the flat and live-in bed-and-breakfast accommodation for a while, until I could find another permanent room.

This bed-and-breakfast arrangement only lasted for a few weeks though and during this confused period, I found myself spending occasional nights sleeping in various places of people that I knew, as well as in shop doorways. This after time in late night cafes making coffee or food last as long as possible.

Before too long, however, some of my hippie friends had invited me to stay with them back in Shepherds Bush. I also changed my job again several times, as I quickly grew fed up with them all.

The accommodation that I had now moved to, was a large four-storey terraced house in a very scruffy rundown part of the area. The man who owned it was a sort of Rachman-type landlord who had converted it into single rooms and even subdivided some of the large rooms to get twice the amount of rent for them. He was quite happy to take on hippies and dropouts, indeed they were the only sort of people who would be prepared to live in such squalid conditions.

I was fully aware at this stage of just how seedy the place was, especially in contrast to the nice clean bed-and-breakfast place which I had left. However, I wanted the company and to be able to listen to records and take drugs quite freely. As the whole house was full of hippies who were all quite friendly with each other, people sometimes swapped around rooms a bit. Apart from staying in the top floor room with the people who had invited me over in the first place, I used to occasionally sleep in another room occupied by Ken and Sheila. They had also moved in and had converted their room into a sort of shrine to Hari Krishna. As a result of being so heavily involved in religion, they were trying now to stop taking drugs, to eat only pure foods and to live cleaner more God-fearing lives as it were.

Once again during this time I tried sleeping with a woman, but all to no avail. Only this time I was largely indifferent about it, as it really didn't seem to matter much anymore.

Meanwhile, there was another group of three or four young men who shared a room in the basement, with whom I had become quite friendly. The conditions in this room were really appallingly filthy and even the blankets had fleas and lice in them. In the condition that I was now in though, none of this really mattered to me and I either sat or lay around completely stoned and almost oblivious to everything.

Once or twice in my saner moments I became increasingly aware of the sordid situation that I had got myself into. I became painfully of this one day, when I met my old friend from Lacton Hall on one of my frequent sorties to Simon and Colin's flat. Having chatted for a while and told him that I was going back to my own place, he volunteered to walk round with me. When we arrived at the door I sat and chatted on the steps with him, not wanting to invite him in as he would see the squalid conditions in which I now lived and the level to which I'd sunk as a person. I could tell during the course of the conversation that I had with him that he realised it anyway and this gave me a bit of a jolt.

Apart from this, even one or two of the people with whom I shared a room had made various comments to me as they could see that I was in a very bad way and genuinely wanted to help. They offered me various pieces of advice and even said that I should give up drugs for a while until I'd sorted myself out. At this stage I was emotionally, mentally and physically shattered. I was also completely confused as to who I was as a person, where I was going, and what, if any, was the point of my life.

However, despite all the advice my friends were trying to give me, I continued taking LSD and amphetamines and also smoking all kind of dope.

Had I continued in this way for very much longer, with little food, not having a job and living in a state of almost constant fear and anxiety, then I quite possibly would not have survived. As it was, during one trip on LSD I suddenly became aware in a very strong personal sense of the existence of God and that line from George Harrison's song hit home really hard.

I saw that I was destroying myself and was in danger of throwing away the life that I had been given. Metaphorically speaking, the Lord kind of picked me up by the scruff of the neck and shook me, to bring me to my senses. I suddenly realised that I had to take personal responsibility for my own life. I knew that whatever else happened, I should now take control and get out of the ghastly state that I had got myself into. The bitter taste of reality that I had so dismally failed to engage with when I left Caldecott, now came back to haunt me and I came to understand the need to repress my negative emotions in order to survive.

So, momentarily, having admitted my error and acknowledged the presence of the existence of God in my life, I felt a flood of warmth and happiness surge through me, which uplifted me for long enough to give me the sense of purpose, which until that point had been sorely lacking. This experience rendered my mind sufficiently clear to enable me to think logically of my next step, which was to revitalise myself physically as soon as I could.

During the previous few months, I'd usually visited my mother about once a week in her room in Richmond for a meal and to spend the evening with her. She, along with Colin and Simon had grown really worried about the way that I was heading and all three probably felt at the back of their minds that at any time the almost inevitable tragic outcome of my life might occur. Indeed, a few months earlier, Simon had encouraged me to watch a documentary called "Gail is Dead", about a girl in care who had died of a heroin overdose. He clearly hoped that it might make a big enough impression on me to change my ways.

My mother, who had been receiving ECT treatment for depression, had now permanently left the various mental hospitals she had been in and out of over the years and was fully embarked on a positive road in life. She had a good job and accommodation and was firmly ensconced in the idea of eating properly and had stopped taking all her medications. She was thus building herself up physically after years of neglecting this area, by eating whole foods and taking vitamin and mineral supplements.

I had been aware of all that she had been doing in that direction, but tended, because of my negative outlook, to pour scorn on all of her ideas. She, in her turn, had been trying to encourage me to eat properly and to stop taking drugs. This had all had no effect on me whatsoever, until one day I arrived at her room and announced that because of my recent experience, I was giving up drugs completely and that I wished to embark on a healthy diet with vitamin pills and could she advise me.

My mother, who was a committed Christian, told me that she had been praying for me during my bad patch and I am convinced that this would have greatly assisted in my realisation of the seriousness of my situation, the subsequent meeting with God and the need to change. She told me of a saying in the Bible that indicates that God takes very close and intimate care of us. I found this to be a great encouragement and it still has a special resonance for me.

This is also borne out very dramatically in my case, in the expression of King David in the Bible, who had gone badly off the rails at one point in his life and was then rescued by the Lord God. He likened this to being pulled out of a slimy pit of mud and mire and being placed on safe, rock-solid ground once more. This fully restored him and gave him great joy.

So, having got my diet sorted out, I now had a burning desire to get out of the filthy and squalid surroundings of the hippie household, with all the attendant unpleasant connotations that it held for me. I wanted to set myself up in a room of my own once again, only this time with a real determination to make a proper go of life and not merely as another phase, which grudgingly had to be entered into.

I discussed all this with my mother and between us we decided it would be best for me to have room near to her in Richmond. This was for two main reasons. Firstly, because it was far removed from the unpleasant associations of inner London, but without being too far to prevent easy access to Colin and Simon. Secondly, because it would mean that I could see plenty of her and as such we would be company for each other. We then set about the task of finding such a room.

Looking back, I think it possible that I had always believed in God, deep down, but for some reason had never acknowledged it, or understood it to be God.

I am also inclined to believe that the reason I went downhill so quickly was because I had really given up hope and when hope is lost everything plummets.

SPRING

Spring

Crocuses nodding gently
in the raw unforgiving breeze,
reaching upwards to the sun
like a group of worshippers
singing praises
to their Creator.

Frogs mate copiously
in the tiny pond,
producing their slippery,
jellied black dots of new life
amid the duckweed.

A statue of Hercules
gazes sightlessly,
uncomprehending
of the beauty at his feet.
Oblivious to nature's vibrant,
ecstatic productivity.

Chapter 31
New Life

Before searching for a room, I had all my hair cut very short and tried to make what clothes I had look as tidy and respectable as possible. My mother and I then embarked once more on the weary trek around in the evenings, looking at newsagents' boards and in the local paper, trying to find something suitable. Before very long our efforts were rewarded and we found a very pleasant house near to where my mother had her room and where the landlord was letting quite comfortable rooms at reasonable rates. The man who was acting as landlord on behalf his daughter who owned the place, was also residing there and was a nice kindly person. He cheerfully showed us round and when I accepted the room, he told me that if there was anything that I needed, I should not hesitate to ask him.

This, of course, was in complete contrast in every way to my previous accommodation and I was really very pleased at this outcome. Also, the proximity of this room to my mother's room was very helpful as it meant that I could call on her each evening, have my supper there and watch television. It also meant that we would be company for each other.

The next step then was to find a job. Initially, we decided that it would be best just to take more or less anything that was on offer in order to earn some money. Then perhaps after a while, I could obtain something that was more rewarding and fulfilling, such as office work of some sort. On the strength of this, I took a job in a local food store and my tasks included filling shelves, operating the till, sweeping the yard and taking in deliveries.

Having achieved both getting a room and a job in a relatively short space of time, I began to feel that I was making definite progress. I was also continuing with both the health foods and the taking vitamin supplements and was, as a result, beginning to feel much better physically. I felt very thankful too, at the way the situation had turned out so happily for me, having been a month or so earlier in a very run down and unhappy state. Now I felt calm and was able to view things in a clearer and more rational way. I began to feel that I wanted to try and give something back, having for so many years just taken everything that was on offer and then squandering it.

I also became aware for the first time of the importance of other people's lives and feelings and not just my own;

feeling as I had done previously, that the world revolved around me and unthinkingly assuming that I was the only person who had problems. I now understood that other people counted too and began to wonder what I could do for them for a change, rather than just the other way around. I couldn't really see what I could do for the world at large, however, but it struck me that the landlord was probably rather lonely with his daughter being abroad most of the time and his wife having died. So occasionally I spent some time chatting to him hoping that he enjoyed the company. This was only a very minor thing of course, but it was the principle involved that counted.

So now, for the first time, I was not only beginning to think of other people, but was taking a realistic approach to the practical problems of life. At the same time, I now fully appreciated not only that I had personal problems, but that if I were to be happy as a person, then I must try and overcome them. This thought was rather daunting, and because I had got myself in such a terrible state, I was unable to identify at that point exactly what my problems were. I knew only that I had been very unhappy and could not relate to people on anything other than a superficial level. So, I felt rather crippled both mentally and emotionally and knew that I was in a mess, but not how to get out of it.

I decided after much thought, therefore, that if I couldn't solve my problems, then I must at least try and learn to live with them. In the meantime, it was vital to maintain a sound and practical approach to life and just keep fighting hard and hoping for the best. Whatever else happened, the most important thing was to remain on an even keel.

After my experience of God and realising that I had to put my life together, I took the view that any hurt that I felt had to be laid aside if I was to make any progress. This "repression" of my feelings was an important safety valve at the time and proved to be a very good way of re-building my life.

From time to time, both Simon and Colin would drop in and visit me in my room and I was always very pleased to see them. On one occasion, Simon called in on his own and I told him how I felt about things and he suggested that perhaps I should have psychotherapy. This was something that had not actually occurred to me, although I knew that Colin had been undergoing psychotherapy for some while. I thought it worth considering, however, for my personality was substantially under-developed at this stage in my life.

Simon also announced on one of his visits that Colin was shortly going to be leaving the flat in Shepherds Bush and was looking around to share a flat with some people of his own age. He asked me if I would like to take Colin's place in the flat and gave me the first option before going elsewhere. I was delighted to have the chance of moving into the flat, which for a long time had been my home, emotionally at least. I really felt that this was a big upturn in my life. Although the previous six months been invaluable in terms of setting myself up on the right road, I had at times found the lack of greater stimulation, other than my mother's company, to be a bit of a gap in my life and I welcomed this opportunity of redressing the balance.

The short time that I had spent with my mother, however, had been so worthwhile, offering as it did, a degree of stability, comfort and the chance to re-build my life. It had been good for her too, as she had prayed for me and had seen a wonderful answer to those prayers. So, the harmony which had not existed in my brief holiday time with her some years before, because of the rows we had, now became a reality. A blessing of God for us both.

Chapter 32
Home at Last

So it was that in March 1972, at the age of 19, that I finally had somewhere to hang my hat, somewhere that I could call home and somewhere where I felt happy and secure. This in an understanding environment that was not only full-time, but equally important, somewhere that was permanent. It was also one that in my new positive state of mind, I could take full advantage of and use constructively in the next stage of my life.

There was another member of the flat, an ex-Caldecott called Matt. He was one of a number of ex-Caldecotts who had occupied a room there over some years previously. Indeed, the flat had been nicknamed by somebody, "Little Caldecott!" Matt and I were very different people, and he had, not surprisingly, found my previous lifestyle to be anathema. He had also had to put up with me being in the flat during my drug days and this clearly hadn't done much to endear him to me! Nonetheless, we now got on well enough, due to my change of heart.

So, having arrived at the flat, I now felt a great sense of responsibility and pleasure at being a rent paying member, albeit a token rent. I felt in some ways that it justified my presence there. In addition, I was contributing in other ways too, like cooking meals. I began to feel also that job-wise I was capable of more than just working in a shop and anyway I was growing very bored with repetitive mundane tasks that I had been doing. I now considered that office work might perhaps suit me better and apart from being more fulfilling, it would ultimately provide me with some sort of career. I had one or two small anxieties as to whether I would be able to cope with this change of emphasis work-wise, but decided to try it out anyway. Before long, having registered with an agency, I managed to obtain a fairly basic clerical job.

The nerve-racking first day came and went and having found that I could cope quite easily with the tasks that had been allotted to me, I felt a glow of pleasure on the way home knowing that I was beginning to make real headway.

I soon began to experience mental conflicts, though, which came to affect my ability to work as well as I should have done. However, I got through these enough to be able to carry on with the job.

A few months later I began to feel that the time was right for me to embark on the course of psychotherapy, that I had earlier discussed with Simon. He was a psychotherapist himself and he put me in touch with a therapist who was going to interview me and then refer me to someone who would give me treatment.

When the interview took place and I sat down to discuss my affairs with him, I found that I could not actually formulate in my mind exactly why I needed it, or indeed exactly how it would help me. Whilst being aware of the principles involved, I could not really identify which areas my personality were not functioning properly, or how I might resolve them just by discussing them with somebody.

I knew that I was in a mess, but couldn't even begin to communicate this adequately to the therapist. He began to question me, ruthlessly it seemed, "Why have you come for therapy?". "What exactly is troubling you?" or questions to that effect. I was simply unable to answer his questions and nothing I said made any real sense. So, I sat in my chair looking across at his searching expectant face, and all I could see was a great yawning chasm between us and worst of all, it was me who had to build the bridge across. I seized up. The gap was too wide. It was like trying to run before I could walk. Fifteen minutes or so passed and then the therapist, having extracted whatever information he could, said that he would refer me to somebody who would be in touch shortly.

When I arrived for my interview with the second therapist, who was a woman, I found that she reminded me of my foster mother and found this rather off putting. Coupled with this, I again found myself helplessly trying to explain why I had come to her and despite the gentler response, the result was the same. I spent much of the hour relating some details of my past history, prompted occasionally by her questions and when it was over, I began to feel that I was not going to get anything out of it and wondered what the best course of action would be.

When I spoke to Simon about it later that evening, he suggested that perhaps it would be wiser not to have any therapy at that point in my life and that I had probably spent far too much time thinking about myself anyway. What I really needed, he felt, was a period of stability, a good home environment with a steady job and a more orderly life with a regular routine. Above all, he said, that I should try and get out of myself and start to enjoy life by going out to theatres, cinemas and restaurants and generally throwing myself into things.

I could certainly see a good deal of sense in this in principle, but felt that it was easier said than done. I had become so introverted over the years, that even the idea of trying to socialise in a normal way seemed virtually impossible. It almost seemed to me that socialising would be a form of escaping from the real me and that if I stopped thinking about how to get out of my predicament, that I would never get out of it.

In fact, the reverse proved to be the case, but it took a long time for me to grasp this. Gradually a part of me began to realise more and more that by putting the hurt and destruction behind me, I could move forward, even if ultimately the pain and confusion inside me could never really be resolved. I had no idea at the time just how long this process would take.

With this in mind, I decided to try what Simon had suggested, just to see. As it turned out, with the sort of person that Simon is, being very lively, jovial and having lots of friends, it became easier than I had at first imagined. Apart from the contacts that I began to develop by meeting his friends who were always dropping in, I also began to accompany him on many of his trips out to their places too. In addition, I joined him on his many outings to theatres, cinemas, concerts and meals out. This began to have a beneficial effect on me in two ways. Firstly, because it took me out of myself and secondly and perhaps more importantly, it began to enlighten me as to how other people thought and felt about things and what they did with their lives.

Ironically, within just a few months of being in the flat, I had a strange dream. I saw a bedraggled cat drowning in a big glass jar. It had a very frightened look in its eyes. Then suddenly, someone pulled it out. Clearly the cat was me and I believe this indicated that in the first instance I was rescued dramatically and spiritually by the Lord God and then emotionally, by Simon.

Interestingly, this is in direct contrast to the feeling of being in a fish tank during my last term at Caldecott, when nobody appeared to notice my condition and I felt as though I was drowning helplessly. Coincidentally, at Caldecott, I was inside the fish tank and desperately looking out, whereas with the cat dream, I was outside the situation and calmly looking in. This, with a wonderful feeling of relief.

What I had needed more than anything was shelter and Simon provided that along with constant emotional warmth, security and fun.

Another really significant and remarkable thought also occurred to me after only a short time of living in the flat. I had this very strong, deep-seated conviction that this friendship with Simon was going to be a rock solid, stable and long-lasting one and thankfully it has proved to be so, after very many happy years. It is mutually supportive, emotionally satisfying, and of tremendous value.

Chapter 33
Gaining Ground

After a while, I began to become aware of yet more new ideas and concepts, which were beginning to change for the better my outlook and perspectives on life. Coupled with this, because of the close personal contact with Simon, I began to feel more secure emotionally as well. At first, when people called round to the flat, apart from the odd one or two that I knew from Caldecott days with whom I could talk quite freely, I was rather withdrawn and nervous, not quite knowing just what I should say to people. Gradually, however, having sat silently and just listened to people on most of these occasions, I was able to make the occasional conversational contribution and slowly warmed up to the spirit of the proceedings.

Many of the friends that Simon had were either social workers, psychotherapists, or people linked in some way to the caring professions. As a result of mixing with these people I became more aware of this vast organisation of people who spent much of their lives helping others. This growing awareness of the social work profession, I found not only interesting, but very reassuring from a human standpoint. To think that here was a body of people who were prepared to give something of themselves to others who really needed it, sometimes at no little cost to themselves, began to give me a more balanced picture of the human race and some personal hope into the bargain.

I also became much more aware of the intricacies of human make- up and the very many different types of people that there are in the world. I saw things not so much in black and white terms, but was able to distinguish other shades in between. I was at last beginning to blossom and grow as a person.

Simon, who came from a very middle-class background, had also experienced his parents' divorce when he was quite young, his father having since remarried. He was still very close to both parents, however, and would often visit each of them at weekends. They both lived in the country about 30 miles outside London and I would accompany him on these visits, very much valuing the chance of getting into the more peaceful environment of the countryside, which I still loved very much.

I was also learning to drive in Simon's car, an MGB GT and these weekend trips gave me a very good opportunity to practice. When I eventually took my test and passed,

Simon's mother very kindly gave me her old car as she had just bought a new one. Apart from this, it was a most interesting experience to see and talk to people who, being that much older, had yet again a very different outlook on life and tended to reflect this in their rather genteel lifestyles. This served to broaden my outlook and attitudes still further.

Simon's Father had run his own business in the Fur Trade for many years and had lived in South Africa and for a time in New York. He was an avid Churchill fan and during his retirement, he was for many years a guide at Chartwell, Churchill's home in Kent. When he stepped down from that, at the age of 80, he wrote a little booklet about Churchill and Chartwell, called "Churchill – Your Questions Answered". It was modestly priced and sold very well during his lifetime, which he was thrilled about, and became their top selling book. Simon took over the ownership and supply to the bookshop there after his father's death and we learned a few years ago that it is now standard issue to all new Guides!

Simon's Mother was at Oxford University in the 1920's and was among the first women to get awarded a degree. When she left, she joined a publishing firm and helped to write a dictionary. Later on, she ran a highly successful nursery school in her home for many years and was a very popular and committed local parish councillor.

Anthony, Simon's brother, ran Tylehurst, which was a Children's home near East Grinstead and helped a great many boys with their problems. He too, like Simon, maintained contact with a number of them after they left and was always available if they needed help of any kind.

One of Simon's Aunts, called Molly, was a lovely, warm-hearted, fun loving lady who had married into the Guinness family. In her younger days she had been a great dancer and along with her husband, Victor, used to win prizes in many a dance competition in the 1920's and 30's. She subsequently learnt to play Bridge and became so proficient at it, that she ultimately taught the game to others. On occasions she played with Omar Sharif! All Simon's family were very kind to me, and I grew very fond of them all over the years.

My contact with my brother Colin at this stage, was minimal, as he was busily involving himself in his new flat and trying to build up his own social life. He was taking out girls and was very much absorbed in all of these activities. I did not really worry about this, however, as I was also absorbed in what I was doing. Overall, things were shaping up very nicely for me and for the first time my life, I was beginning to feel some consistent inner satisfaction and contentment.

After a few months of my living in the flat, Simon decided to buy his own house and started to look around at various places. I joined him on his house hunting excursions and before long we found a house a few miles from Shepherds Bush, which we both took to at once and with hardly any hesitation he put in an offer. Before long, the house purchase was complete and we moved in, along with Matt, the third member of the flat. Later, Matt moved out of the house into his own flat. After that, a number of other ex-Caldecotts came and lived with us, and also moved on, so we then had the place to ourselves.

Chapter 34
Moving On

The move took place in late autumn of 1972, and apart from being a very pleasant house and nicely situated, it was also within walking distance of my place of work and the move overall was a very pleasing state of affairs as far as I was concerned. Matt was also pleased about the move and he and I were beginning to build up quite a good friendship, having started off at opposite ends of the spectrum!

Shortly after the move, Colin announced that he had met someone very special and wanted to introduce us all to her. So, we fixed an evening for him to call round and he then introduced us to Maureen, a very warm-hearted girl and we all chatted away and then went out for a drink. During the course of the evening, we decided we would all go on a skiing holiday in Austria. This holiday proved to be a great success and was the start of many more trips abroad for Simon and me, either on our own, or with other people.

A few months after this holiday, Colin announced that he was getting married and this took place in November of 1973. I remember thinking to myself at that point, that now he was married, the first and foremost person in his life would quite naturally be his wife, Maureen. I deliberately and quite readily accepted this, feeling as I did, that although for many years we had subconsciously held a very special place in each other's lives, the strong bond that we had forged between us had receded somewhat, as we both of us now felt quite secure in our own ways and thus had less need of it.

We still maintain a very good relationship, although we are fairly different personalities. Over the years since the birth of his four children, I proudly and happily accepted the role of both uncle and Godfather. This has been a most enlightening experience in that it was a complete role reversal, and I was now in a position, although not directly as a parent, to influence and contribute to the children's happiness and well-being, however modest that was.

This realisation of the responsibility that we have as adults towards children had a profound effect on me, seeing as I did, how young children totally rely and depend on adults, believing virtually anything they were told, at least in the early years, and trusting implicitly in the adults' integrity. I began to see just how easy it is to damage a child's life by ill treatment or neglect.

Conversely, by providing them with a just, loving and caring environment, it can give them the sort of start in life that will enable them to love, grow and freely build relationships with others. This helps them to find the sort of fulfilment and happiness we all desire and need, as well as enabling them to contribute to others and society in general. I could now view life from both the child's and the adult's point of view.

I also have a close relationship with my eldest brother, Dennis, and with my nieces and all of their children. This is a great source of joy to me.

Thus, the years began to roll happily past, bringing with them much in the way of learning and fulfilment. The many trips that I took abroad on holiday with Simon were not only exciting and enjoyable but enlightening too, particularly in relation to seeing the many different cultures and political systems. The countries that I visited during this time among others, were China, Hong Kong, Russia, Greece, Morocco, France, Turkey and Italy.

After about six years, the publishing firm that I worked for merged with another, and I felt the need to move on. So, I obtained a job in another much smaller magazine publishing company nearby. The money was better here and I had more responsible tasks. After a while, though, I began to realise that office work was not my forte and so I gave it up and did mini-cab driving for a bit whilst I thought out what to do next.

Then I hit upon the idea of running a small mail order business from home, which did quite well to start with, but wasn't sustainable in the long term. Then after a period of being unemployed, a local handyman, who had done work for us and was a real stalwart in the local community, said I could work with him on his building and decorating jobs. He taught me how to decorate and this all went really well.

One of the people we worked for was a very nice lady and at some point, she asked me if I would like to tidy up her garden for her. I agreed, although I didn't have much interest in gardening or that much knowledge either. However, as so often happens, I caught the "Gardening Bug" very quickly. Then to my surprise the lady next door popped her head over the fence one day and asked me if I would do her garden for her, to which I happily agreed. This became a kind of domino effect and over the months ahead I took on other gardens purely through word of mouth and so my gardening business took off!

So, in the spring, summer and autumn I did gardening and in the quiet winter months, started decorating and building wardrobes and cupboards in some of the houses that I did gardening for. Thus began a very satisfying and fulfilling line of work which lasted for over 30 years and gave me great joy. I always got on well with the people I worked for and it suited me incredibly well. If I had said to someone that I wanted a job which "ticked all the boxes", then this would have been it, although I had no inkling that this line of work would be so ideal for me. It just dropped out of the blue, straight into my lap and I thank God for all that it has meant to me.

So this gardening work apart from giving me confidence in myself and raising my self-esteem, it also helped me to begin to understand more the mechanics of relationships and the joys and benefits of them. All this in addition to just hugely enjoying the nature of the work. Also, crucially for me, giving me the time and space to reflect. Years later, as a result of this, poems and ideas would come to me and I would jot them down in my little notepad and develop them later on. In an office job that would have been impossible. So, I am very grateful to the Lord God for creating this wonderful job opportunity for me, which suited me so very well and lasted for so long, until I retired, in fact. It exactly suited my personality and needs.

When I was 25, I inherited some money from my father's estate and Simon and I together, bought a fabulous cottage in Suffolk. Over many years we enjoyed wonderful holidays there and also let other people use it too.

When Simon retired, we got the first of many delightful dogs who have been a great joy to us over the decades.

In 1983 the Caldecott Community was trying to raise a substantial sum of money to build new housing especially geared to very emotionally damaged children. So, they held a fundraising event in the Cholmondeley Room in the House of Lords. The chair of trustees at that time was Lord Brabourne and I imagine that he secured this room for the event. The Archbishop of Canterbury at the time was Robert Runcie and he was the Patron of the Caldecott Community. So, he was also present amongst various other dignitaries. Also attending were several representatives of charitable foundations, in the hope that they would make donations to this important cause.

Amongst other speakers, two ex-Caldecotts were asked to speak about what Caldecott had done for them and I was privileged to be one of them. I spent a good deal of time preparing my speech and as the time drew near to give it, I began to grow rather nervous and this was especially so on the day itself. This was heightened, as it was the first occasion that I had done any public speaking. The thought of standing up in front of all these people and giving my talk was very daunting, especially given the somewhat emotional nature of the subject matter.

I had prayed about this event, though, and as I stood up in my nervous state, I had a very powerful image of a kind of imaginary railing or barrier that sprang up and shielded me from all those people present in a most remarkable way. My anxiety disappeared and I felt completely protected. So, by the grace of God, I was able to give my talk successfully and I hope that it made a worthwhile contribution to the proceedings.

Thus, life carried on in this happy way and ultimately, after the death of Simon's father and later on his mother in 1994, we began to spend more of our weekends at home. So, as a result of my belief in God, that I had first encountered some years before, I felt after a while, that it would be good to join a local Church. Simon agreed and after trying one or two in the area, we finally settled on one which we took to straight away. We attended this regularly and then became members on the Electoral Role and have never looked back. This Church then began to play a pivotal role in my life, going forward.

SUMMER

Letter to Heaven

Lord, you are a wondrous God.
If I give all my problems to you,
you can deal with them.
You receive hurtful memories and a troubled spirit
and draw them to you.
You reassure me that you are taking care of them,
and as if that wasn't enough,
you exchange them for joy and peace,
whilst you are repairing and restoring them.

I am glad.
in fact, I am overjoyed,
because whilst I experience that serenity,
you free my mind and my spirit,
to concentrate on serving you.
You bless me five times over
from one simple act of faith on my part.

Lord you are a bountiful God.
Whilst I am serving you, you give me rest
in showing me the beautiful things in the world.
Who else but you, would invest a speck of pollen
with such beauty in its form and colour?
And as if that wasn't enough it helps
produce a wonderful plant as well,
which is a miracle in itself.

Lord, you are an amazing God.
You haven't just designed and empowered me,
and specks of pollen. But you have done so
for all of humanity, whether they know it or not.
You have designed trees and birds and animals
in the most incredible variety and detail.
For our enjoyment, you have made many colours,
where one, or none, would have sufficed.
You created food in many textures and flavours,
which you did not need to do.

Lord, you are a marvellous God.
You run the entire universe,
always have, and always will do,
and yet you can still find time for me.

Lord, I could go on telling you forever
of all the wonderful things
that you have created and done.
The gift of music, of touch,
or the beautiful scent of a flower.
The joy of human friendship and laughter.
The priceless gift of prayer.
The list is endless.

So, Lord, when I ponder on all of these things,
it is then that I realise why you are so infinitely worthy
of our praise and worship.

So, I just want to thank you for being
who you are
and I want to thank you for creating me as I am,
and for making this world such a beautiful
and amazing place in which to live.

And all of this is what you are doing for us now.
Let alone eternity…..

Lord, you are a wondrous God.

Chapter 35
Going to Church

The Church we had now joined was a very warm and welcoming one and we soon became more involved in their activities. This proved to be a great step forward for me. I began to take on various roles and I was both surprised and delighted that people should have the confidence in me to do them and that I had the confidence in myself. For I had never really taken on anything much in the way of responsible roles in an organisation before.

Among these roles was editing the internal Church Magazine for several years. In addition, I did stewarding duties and for a while was elected on to the PCC. I also helped to start up a "Prayer Chain" to offer payer support for anyone in the congregation who needed it and I became more conscious of a sense of duty to serve God and use any gifts that I possessed for that purpose.

Although I had been baptised when I was a baby, I had never been confirmed and decided to have confirmation classes to put this right. When the time came for my confirmation to take place it should have been done by the diocesan Bishop. However, there was an interregnum at the time, so I had the enormous privilege of being confirmed at St Paul's Cathedral by Richard Chartres, then Bishop of London. My family attended, and it was a very special occasion indeed.

Thus, I was grateful for the progress that I was making personally. However, I still lacked any real ambition. So, when I reached my late forties, I experienced a sort of a mid-life crisis. I knew that I still had unresolved hurt from my early years and really felt that I had not achieved anything of any great significance up to that point and wanted to do more.

Also, perhaps, not surprisingly, I had suffered from various mental health issues over the years and Simon supported me through them.

Once when I was going through some old letters and having a clear out, I came across some from my aunt Evelyn, who by now had died. I thought I would discard them, so I tore them up and was about to throw them away, when I had a kind of gut reaction. It felt like I was tearing up and throwing away a piece of myself and I couldn't do it. I then pieced them all together again and stuck them with Sellotape. It wasn't till some years afterwards, that I was finally able to discard them. Clearly this was symptomatic of much that was still unresolved in me emotionally. I guess these feelings were enhanced due to the simple words of comfort she had offered me at my father's funeral many years earlier.

Also, I have long had mixed feelings about carols, much as I love them. This is because they used to take me straight back to my childhood and the time of turmoil that I experienced then, although as time has passed, these emotions have substantially faded. However, there is still occasionally a wistful, almost subconscious longing, to go back there, to want to make things better in a way that cannot be done; to continue and develop relationships that were cut off.

In the following poem I tried to capture these mixed emotions.

In Dulci Jubilo.

(In sweet rejoicing)

In sweet rejoicing, yes,
but also, bittersweet.
O Little Town...... in which
the silent stars do not go by,
I find myself walking in the lanes
with my mother,
near the farm in evening starlight.

All in a half-remembered tiny tot haze.

It haunts me.

We Three Kings in the chapel.
Heartfelt choir boy solo:
**Sorrowing, sighing, bleeding,
dying.**

It haunts me still.

As with Gladness.....I see the
elderly Quaker lady
and hear again
her inspirational talks.
I see two girls as they
read aloud the Gospel tidings.
I re-live the Christmas party
and see, so often, the
mammoth Christmas tree.

It is then, that **Hark**,
I hear **the Herald Angels**
mournfully sing their
would be joyful news to me.

This **Silent Night** not so silent now,
as these unshakeable images

offer no comfort
In the bleak midwinter
of my ghostly past.

An amorphous blend of memories.
My mother, father, my friends,
Margaret and John.
A land to which we none of us
can ever return.

O that we were there
to bend more joyful footsteps
O..... that we were there.

However, we cannot recreate the past, but it can be transformed and good can come out of it if we learn lessons and forgive. This may never obliterate the memories, but it will make them increasingly fade and become a brighter future. This process may be difficult to achieve, but it can be made much easier if we draw on the power of God, for he indicates in the Bible that he will restore any lost and wasted years that we may have experienced.

Healing is a long-term process and much can and does happen in the here and now, but we will none of us achieve perfection in any areas of our lives this side of heaven.

R.D. Laing, the well-known psychiatrist, believed that mental illness was a normal reaction to abnormal circumstances. This may not be the case with all forms of mental illness, but there is a good deal of truth in it as far as I can see. The mind and emotions must react to outside stimuli, or indeed lack of stimuli, in some way shape or form. A healthy stimulus must surely produce a healthy reaction and vice versa.

So, I still clearly had unresolved emotional deprivation and felt the time had maybe come to deal with it. Apart from a few people that knew about my past, I had not told anyone about it, as I did not think it relevant or appropriate to do so. However, after a few years of being a Church member, I had an increasing feeling that I should talk with the Vicar, with a view to telling my life story. He took up this idea and it was arranged that I should use the sermon slot at two services to relate the story in a very condensed form. This was not an easy thing to do. Nonetheless, I did it and the impact on the congregation was very significant.

I thus had a strong sense that the Lord had bandaged me up for many years to sustain me, but the time had now come for him to remove the bandages and heal the remainder of the wounds.

So, I asked for some healing prayer.

Chapter 36
Healing

Broken Lives

The world is full of broken lives,
of birds who never learned to fly,
their precious fledging bodies
lying vulnerable as prey.

The world is full of broken glass,
lacerating all who walk across it unawares.
Painful, bleeding feet, crippling
otherwise healthy, productive bodies

The world is full of people with mental scars
whose capacity to think and feel
in normal, tender creative human ways
is blighted, leaving only disturbed, unhappy visions.

The world is full of beauty,
untouched and untrammelled by human destruction.
A beauty that speaks of healing and grace,
and brings us to the feet of Jesus in awe and wonder.

The world is full of the healing breath of God,
of his infinite power, compassion and love,
that mends the broken wings, binds the bleeding feet
and tenderly heals the scarred, distorted mind.

Repression is a very good and necessary form of coping with painful experiences. It enables us to survive and have some semblance of normality in life, by acting as a form of self-defence. Thus, it becomes possible to function in varying degrees.

Nonetheless, in the long term, it can become counter-productive in that good and positive emotions cannot be properly expressed. In other words, it blunts the emotions, curbs creativity and thereby diminishes the overall quality of life. That is why healing becomes desirable or even necessary.

However, this process requires the re-surfacing of untreated pain that has remained buried, perhaps for many years. This can play havoc with one's emotions and render it very difficult, at least in the short term to live in a stable way. This is primarily because it becomes unavoidable to lose some degree of control over them in order to heal them.

So, this process is not necessarily good for everyone as it can potentially do more harm than good. Each person is different in terms of the depth of deprivation, or indeed abuse, and it needs to be done very carefully. For some it will need professional help from qualified psychotherapists. I suppose it really needs a kind of risk/benefit analysis of some kind to determine whether it is right to embark on treatment or not. For those who have faith, prayer about it all is, in my view, essential.

For me it was like opening a "Pandora's Box" of emotions. I felt a mixture of hope mixed with depression and the inevitable loss of control to a certain extent. Nonetheless, I knew all along, that for me it was the right thing to do and this was because of the faith that I had in God and his guidance. This was corroborated by those offering the healing prayer.

So, this healing took the form of Prayer Counselling and consisted of several sessions. During one of these, one of the healers said to me that God can heal our subconscious without our even knowing it. I then had an almost comical image of God nipping round behind me and twiddling with the back of my head. My immediate reaction was one of deep cynicism.

But that is exactly what happened and in a way that I cannot explain, I underwent a radical change in my perception of things as a result of these prayer sessions. And although they were very painful for me at the time, they did produce the most amazing results.

I experienced a kind of creative explosion within me and I began to write poetry of all kinds. I then produced five little booklets of poems over the next few years. These were used in a modest way to help raise funds for the Church and a local charity. I also became the "Poet in Residence" on my local paper and regularly displayed my poems in a local café. I even wrote a couple of hymns that were sung in Church at different times.

In addition, I started a little entertainment and arts club, called "The Vortex" with the help of other Church members. We put on concerts in the Church, and mounted art exhibitions in various locations. I wrote two short dramas, which were also staged in Church and started to take more interest in other people and the world generally. This was a huge surprise to me and a very significant progression.

Apart from anything else, this substantially boosted my sense of self-worth and gave me a real sense of purpose. It also released the emotional side of my life and enabled me to act with much more confidence within my Christian faith. Thus, the relationship between the spiritual side and the human/emotional side of life became more balanced and my personality became far more integrated, and I got life in a better, healthier perspective. Father God simply dissolved many of my mental fears and frailties. He has helped me to become more adaptable, flexible and spontaneous, for which I offer him my everlasting gratitude.

It was during these sessions that the following poem came to me in the middle of the night. I jotted it down in a notebook that I keep by my bed, for I knew it would be lost by morning if I didn't. I called it "FLYING UNDER THE RADAR" and it highlights the way that God, and indeed people, can sometimes break through our defences and create or re-create a relationship. This is especially so where trust has broken down.

Flying under the Radar

You go to the very core of me,
where no-one else can go.
You slipped in under the radar,
you were flying so dangerously low.

But it wasn't till I saw
the sunlight glinting on your wing,
that I could see you weren't the enemy
and it was safe to let you in.

A passage in the Bible gives substance to this in a remarkable way. It says that God has great plans for us, so that we might have hope and a rewarding and life enhancing future.

So, as the years went by, I came to understand increasingly, that whatever happens to us, we have not only to take responsibility for our own lives, but that good can come out of bad experiences, if we are able to act positively towards them. God can make that possible.

All in all, I now have very positive outlook on life and look forward to the future as being a time of exciting challenge. I have many goals and ambitions which at one time just didn't exist for me, and I'm now able to look at my life and try and improve my performance in every area.

For years I had been looking through the window of other's lives and had not only seen how they live them, but have been invited to take part. By so doing, I have come to learn what it means to feel warm and secure. I've slowly crawled out from the cold starkness that was my isolation and I now feel that I'm a part of life and not just a helpless bystander.

Me

I have discovered me.
Here I am.
Actually, I was here all the time,
for all those years,
but I just didn't know it.

Now I can relate to myself.
And so can others too
if I will let them.

I like being me.
It feels good.
It feels like I just met someone
I've known for years,
but didn't know they
lived in the same street as me.

Here I am.
I like me.
I hope you like me too,
whoever you are.
Together we can have
so much fun and joy
and laughter.

Life is so much nicer,
when you know who you are.
I am real,
I know I am real.
Life is no longer a sideshow
seen from the window
of an isolated, empty world.
I am part of it now.

As things now stand, I am a survivor. I have lived through very difficult experiences and by the Grace of God and the help and support of my fellow human beings, have come through them. I have learned to accept my shortcomings and be patient as I try slowly to overcome them. I have learned the importance of give-and-take and also to consider other people's thoughts and feelings as well as my own.

I have learned too, the lesson that you have to put something into life before you can get anything out of it and that ultimately everybody has to conform to the realities of life, however hard it has hit them or difficult they may be.

This has been a long, slow and sometimes painful process, but well worth the learning. I now consider myself to be a relatively well-adjusted human being, who can contribute to society and at the same time enjoy living.

Epilogue

In time of difficulty

By my mother, Diana Inwood.

There is no grief or heartache that God does not understand,
There is no life, placed in his care, escapes his guiding hand.
There is no kind act done, no matter whether great or small,
That he does not remember, for he knows about it all.

There is no pain or sorrow, doubt or fear, or heavy load,
With which we have to struggle as we journey on life's road,
That he did not know well before our journey was begun,
For he had human feelings in the person of his Son.

There is no sense of failure, or frustration, or despair,
That He will not dispel, if we will contact him in prayer.
There is no discipline of self, He'll not reward at length,
And help our faltering efforts, with the power of His strength.

There is no disappointment that He will not help us through,
Until we see His plan for us unfold when it is due.

There is no faith and trust in him that ever was betrayed,
For with blood of His dear Son for all our sins he paid.

There is no brave endurance of the hardship of this life,
Or conquering of bitterness, rebellion and of strife;
Of weariness and hopelessness, escapes His deep compassion,
We, out of these things, a stronger character will fashion.

There is no yearning of the heart, unknown to him who came,
Into this troubled world of ours and took our human frame.
He shared this human life of ours; He knows all our desires.
He will not leave us comfortless; His mercy never tires.

There is no dark horizon that forever will remain,
For daylight, warmth and sunshine follow darkness,
cold and rain.
Though we pass through the darkest hours,
the promise of the dawn,
Is always there to give us hope, before the night is gone.

In the intervening years of my living with Simon, my mother held several different jobs as a typist and moved rooms several times. When she retired, she moved down to Eastbourne and during her time there enjoyed singing in a bar on a regular basis. She then moved back to London, near to my brother Colin and latterly to a room very near to Simon and me. During those years she saw a great deal of my eldest brother Dennis and enjoyed being with my brother, Colin and his family of four girls. I, too, saw her frequently and we all grew much closer as a family, which was a great joy.

As she grew older, her memory started to deteriorate and we eventually found her a place in a care home near to my brother Dennis. Before long she became increasingly frail and confused and died in July 1997. Dennis was with her soon after she died and said that she looked beautiful and had a very peaceful look on her face.

Her funeral was held in a Church near to Dennis, an area where she had lived as a child, during her years at Coldridge Farm and for some years afterwards.

O Lord of Mercy

By my father, Cyril Inwood.

O Lord whose mercy, love and power,
Cam save us from our sins,
Be our Good Shepherd ever near,
To make us all true friends.

Give us great faith to make us whole,
And humble from the heart.
Thy wisdom show where we have failed,
And in our hearts atone.

When all in life seems really lost,
Our faith in Thee is waning,
In sorrow may we ever know,
Thy great love will prevail.

That helping where the need is great,
The lonely and the old,
Thy children who are in the homes,
May know a Father's love.

When in Thy world they have to strive,
Please bless them in their work.
Be Thou their guide for evermore,
A union without end.

When my father came out of mental hospital he initially bought and lived in a caravan and worked for a while as a gardener for the hospital in a voluntary capacity. I think this must have helped him in his recovery, because after a while he sold the caravan and bought himself a very nice bungalow called "St Martin's". This had a good-sized garden, the tending of which gave him much pleasure. In fact, on a visit to my father to discuss various issues relating to Colin and me, our Child Care Officer noted that his garden was "Immaculate".

He also took in a tenant with whom he became quite friendly and on occasions took him and his fiancé out for little day trips, as they did not have a car. My brother, Colin's and my relationships with him flourished to a reasonable degree during this time, which was a great blessing. He also came to London on occasions and went out for meals with Colin and Simon (I was still at school), which he thoroughly enjoyed. So, he lived in "St Martin's" in a reasonably happy state for his last few remaining years. He died in 1968 aged 60.

Dear Mum and Dad

I felt I had to write;
to square things up,
and put you both
in the picture.

Your frequent rows
caused each other
much hardship
and suffering.

Dad, your behaviour
went beyond the bounds
of human dignity.
This not only hurt us,
but stole your life
away from you,
didn't it?

Mum, your strong-willed,
determined character,
railed against my dad
and his attitudes
and wore you down.
You had less and less energy
to meet our needs.

Your marriage
was a result
of two people
whose lives crossed
in somewhat unhappy
circumstances.

Neither of you meant us harm;
but our lives, our emotions
became the unintended victims
of your problems
and cast a dark shadow over us
for years.

You left us rooted in bewilderment
and passed us on to others
to try and pick up the pieces.

Whatever happened
to your Christian faith?

In the end you never
really lost it, did you,
in those, miserable
guilt-ridden years that,
were the cruel aftermath
of a broken,
traumatised family?

But they are all over now.
You have forgiven
and been forgiven.

So, too, have I.

One day I shall see you again.
I will share your lives once more.
But this time we will all be
in perfect harmony.

Forever.

Printed in Great Britain
by Amazon

47412220R00159